Oban
and the
Land of Lorn

compiled by
Christopher J. Uncles

By the same author:

Last Ferry to Skye
Lochaber and the Road to the Isles
Easter Ross and the Black Isle
Old Ways Through Wester Ross

Formerly one of the great manufacturing industries of Lorn, the Bonawe Iron Furnace required immense amounts of wood to create charcoal, a vital ingredient in the smelting process.
(Picture reproduced from an engraving of 1836 entitled 'Benawe, Loch Etive, from near Taynuilt'.)

Stenlake Publishing
2001

FOREWORD

Ask a number of Argyll residents what they understand to be the geographical extent of the Land of Lorn, and it is likely that several quite divergent and conflicting suggestions will emerge. It is evident that authors, too, have their differing emphases, some including parts of the area which others may surprisingly neglect. However, authorities generally seem to agree that the boundaries are somewhat arbitrary, so for the purposes of this book I have adopted the broadly accepted view that the essentials of this area are bounded to the north and south by Loch Leven and Loch Craignish respectively, to the east by Loch Awe and on the west by the Firth of Lorn.

 Oban and the Land of Lorn, consisting mainly of postcards and photographs from my own collection dating from the 1880s to the 1930s, is divided into three sections: Inverary to Port Appin; Oban – Glen Nant – Ford; and Oban to Dunadd. Each is preceded by an introduction. I am also pleased to include an appreciation of the work of the late H. M. Scrivens of Oban, who recorded with his camera so many scenes which now constitute such an important contribution to the local history of the area. Tragically, his own photographic archive has failed to survive, and it is to photographs and postcards in private collections that we must turn in order to appreciate his legacy.

Christopher J. Uncles

ACKNOWLEDGEMENTS

H. M. Scrivens: Over a number of years, several residents were good enough to provide snippets of information on Scrivens' early life in Oban, but I am especially indebted to Mrs Mary Thompson for lending the photograph of H.M.S., to Iain Nicolson who kindly copied it, and to *The Oban Times* for permission to reproduce it here, together with extracts from the obituary originally carried by that newspaper. Murdo MacDonald (Archivist, Argyll and Bute Council) located the 1926 plan for the studio enlargement, and was immensely helpful in confirming other details.

 Elsewhere, for Robin Buchanan-Smith of Eriska nothing was too much trouble, and I am grateful for his pointing me in the right direction on occasions, and for lending the photograph of the Connel Bridge under construction.

 To Jean Adams MBE (Curator, Easdale Island Folk Museum) and Robert McCulloch of Oban for photographs, and to John Martin who contributed much to the history of quarrying at Bonawe. As before, Angela typed the manuscript from my handwritten pages and provided so much help in other ways, and, once again, Oliver van Helden of Stenlake Publishing used his technical wizardry to fit the complex jigsaw together. Thank you all.

© Christopher J. Uncles 2001
First published in the United Kingdom, 2001,
by Stenlake Publishing, Ochiltree Sawmill, The Lade,
Ochiltree, Ayrshire, KA18 2NX
Telephone / Fax: 01290 423114
www.stenlake.co.uk

ISBN 1 84033 138 0

HENRY MORTON SCRIVENS of OBAN

Pictures from the past invariably evoke nostalgia, but an old photograph has much greater significance than the mere ability to reawaken memories of earlier years. It is, arguably, the purest form of social document, the most valuable record of days long gone – better by far than the partial and fallible memory of old age, or the most descriptive prose. Click! The camera shutter has operated and another image has been captured on film. Many of the images shown between these pages appeared on early postcards issued by small publishing firms whose names have long since vanished, and of whom virtually nothing is known. Often even less is known about the all-important photographer who stood behind the camera to create the picture. Of course, there are exceptions, and of those who photographed the Scottish Highlands and Islands some even achieved national recognition during Queen Victoria's reign, while others came to prominence at the turn of the twentieth century. Up until the Great War, the firm of McIsaac and Riddle was a household name in Oban, their shop on the Esplanade being a familiar port of call for residents and tourists alike. Shortly after the end of the war, the town would be fortunate to see the appearance of another such business which, both photographically and professionally speaking, would effectively carry the torch lit by McIsaac and Riddle for the next four decades, producing a body of work which would become a priceless portrayal of life and events around the locality. What follows is the story of that 'photographic life'.

On a day in early June 1973 following a service in St Columba's Church, Argyll Square, relatives, friends and Oban residents gathered at Pennyfuir Cemetery to pay their last respects to a locally well-known man who at the conclusion of the Great War had adopted this part of western Argyll as his home. An Englishman by birth, he had distinguished himself as a professional photographer of the Oban area over a period of some 40 years. Officially noted in the records at Pennyfuir as 'Harry M. B. Scrivens (aged 79 years)', he was better known locally simply as Henry Scrivens.

Regrettably, several potential lines of enquiry to relatives came to naught owing to the passage of time, and while I have not researched Scrivens' very early life, it is known that as a young man he served a photographic apprenticeship in Doncaster. His brother, Edgar Leonard Scrivens (who died about 1950), had been a noted photographer in that Yorkshire town, and I am told examples of his work are keenly sought by collectors.

During the Great War, Scrivens, then in his early twenties, found himself aboard the former Granton trawler *Newhaven* on minesweeping duties down the length of the Scottish west coast. His ship, with others, was based in Stornoway, and periodically this necessitated putting into Oban for coaling and to give the crew shore leave. During his wartime service he continued to take an active interest in photography, taking a number of dramatic pictures depicting conflict at sea, including one of a mine exploding near his ship. This photograph appeared on the front page of the *Illustrated London News*, earning him 25 guineas, a princely sum in those days.

As can be imagined, naval personnel eagerly anticipated shore leave at Oban after lengthy spells at sea, and a popular attraction was Cinema House (later the Phoenix) at the northern end of George Street. Leaving the cinema after an evening performance, Scrivens made what subsequently proved to be a fateful decision. Instead of turning left to return to his ship moored at the Railway Pier, he turned right and into the Sailors and Soldiers Rest for a meal in the canteen. This seemingly mundane variation to his normal route ultimately shaped the whole of his future life. The Great War was moving towards its close, and surveying the canteen, Scrivens reflected thoughtfully on the future and how suitable these premises would be if converted to a photographic studio. He resolved, there and then, that when hostilities ended he would try to purchase this site and set up business on his own account. When the peace eventually came, and upon his discharge from the Navy, that is precisely what he did! He made Oban his home, and is first listed on the electoral roll in 1921. Utilising his naval gratuity to assist with the costs of acquisition and conversion, he at last had his own studio and would be able to pursue his chosen occupation in civilian life.

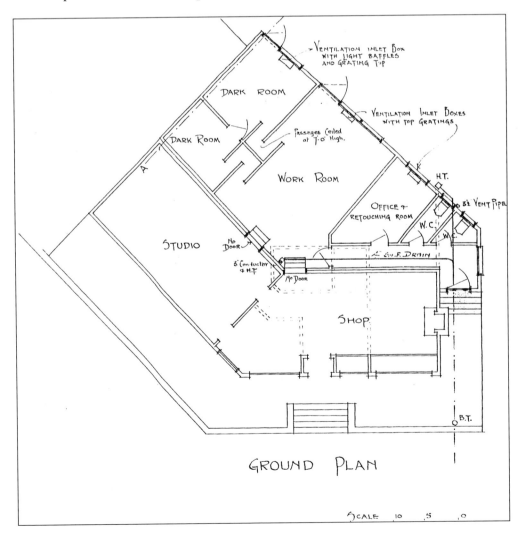

GROUND PLAN

After the war, tourists gradually began to return to Oban in numbers. From quite humble origins the studio at the junction of Nursery Lane and George Street (later numbered 130 George Street), underwent a series of transformations to increase capacity as business flourished. The valuation roll for 1922–1923 described the premises simply as a 'stance for studio and wooden building'. In 1922 Scrivens applied for permission to build a darkroom, but four years later he had much more ambitious plans for expansion which would practically double the size of the existing premises by adding two darkrooms, a workroom, and an office and retouching room at the rear. Said by some to be somewhat tongue-in-cheek, the words Maison de Photographie were mounted above the entrance. Henry Scrivens' neighbour, Mrs Mary Thompson, knew the studio well in its heyday when the business employed a staff of fourteen. Work undertaken included formal studio portraiture (there must still be many who have a Scrivens picture of themselves taken as children tucked away in a family photograph album), film processing for individuals and for three branches of Boots the Chemists (Oban, Lochgilphead and Ardrishaig), the sale of his own local view postcards and photographs, picture framing – and, there was even a fine art section (see also page 59).

However, some of Scrivens' most enduring work is not to be found in the formal poses required for studio work, but in his role as a roving mobile photographer where his subjects could be caught on camera spontaneously. He recorded people at work and at play and many local social events, including scenes at the annual Oban Games, where he would photograph not only competitors but also sections of the crowd. Afterwards people would flock to the Maison de Photographie (later known simply as 'The Studio') to examine his photographs, displayed in the windows and on the counter, attempting to identify themselves. Some of his

H. M. SCRIVENS

PHOTOGRAPHER & ARTIST

FILMS DEVELOPED AND PRINTED EFFICIENTLY AND PROMPTLY. DARK ROOMS for use of Clients.

All KODAK Supplies and Accessories.

Etchings and Water Colours by noted Artists.

Wireless Sets, Valves and Batteries.

130 GEORGE STREET - - OBAN

pictures appeared in the national press, including images of PS *Grenadier* which was fatally destroyed in a disastrous fire at the North Pier in 1927, just one of a number of examples of his work featured in this book.

The body of work produced by Scrivens over his lifetime was prodigious, and he left a superb photographic legacy of what might be termed 'the greater Oban area', including Mull and Iona. Further afield, scenes up the coast to what was then the Ballachulish ferry, Kilchoan in Ardnamurchan and Scapa Flow in the Orkneys featured in his work, while just recently I noted a picture he had taken in Glen Lyon (Perthshire).

Henry Morton Scrivens retired in 1958 and, although he had a number of local interests, these did not altogether compensate sufficiently for his former active business life. He soon became restless, and Alan E. Cameron of *The Oban Times* offered him part-time employment in the paper's developing and printing room, this work continuing until three months before his death on 31 May 1973. Without exception, those who knew Scrivens personally spoke warmly of him and testify to the high regard in which he was held. His enduring memorial will be his photographs, many taken in the field which survive as postcards, often selling for a few pence in the early days. The selection of his material included in this book from my own collection is offered by way of a personal tribute to a man who photographically-speaking helped to put Oban on the map. By a twist of fate, the former Scrivens' studio has reverted to a catering establishment of one form or another in recent years. As I write, Oban somewhat surprisingly has no museum devoted to the area which it serves as 'capital'. How appropriate it would be if perhaps the former studio premises could be acquired to house a small museum for the town. Now there's a thought . . .

INVERARY to PORT APPIN

Down the ages, westbound travellers have entered the lands of Lorn through the natural defiles of Glen Lochy and Glen Orchy, or from Loch Fyne and Inverary to the south by way of Glen Aray. The present road system has largely developed from tracks originally used by drovers, pilgrims or the military. A number of 'green roads', the old routes over which drovers moved their cattle, criss-crossed the area. Several of these varied routes on the eastern boundary of Lorn had one aspect in common; they converged around the head of Loch Awe near Dalmally and Stronmilichan, which lie opposite each other across the River Orchy in the strath of the same name. There the Dalmally trysts were held; historically these Glenorchy fairs took place at Martinmas and Michaelmas. Dated 1734, one of the earliest (and possibly the oldest) maps of the Argyll dukedom shows a track from the east which takes the general line of the present-day A85 road from Dalmally through to Bonawe on Loch Etive. Making use of the straths, glens and passes, the construction of the new Callander and Oban Railway followed a similar direction as it pushed westwards in the 1870s.

For early travellers by road, their route under the towering heights of Ben Cruachan and through the rough, narrow and inhospitable Pass of Brander, from which the sun is largely excluded, would have been a gloomy and often grim experience, especially in winter. It was not until the middle of the eighteenth century that the River Awe was bridged, and until that time the road followed the right (east) bank of the river down to its mouth at Bonawe. Here the journey would necessarily continue by ferry, either over the Awe for Taynuilt and the west, or northwards across Loch Etive. There would have been much visible activity on either side of the loch, as two of the most important former industries of Lorn were located hereabouts – the Lorn Iron Furnace and the Bonawe Quarries. On the north side of Loch Etive, the road kept close to the shoreline (as does its present-day counterpart), heading west past the former Valliscaulian priory at Ardchattan, and skirting the slopes of Ben Lora to reach Port Selma in Benderloch. Having reached the lands of Benderloch and Appin, those on the road could continue up the coast to Lismore or the Ballachulish narrows by making use of a number of small rowboat ferries, which plied between remote jetties avoiding time-consuming inland detours. These were complemented by ferry-boat inns where very basic hospitality was on offer. Among these ferry routes, South Shian to North Shian was but one crossing Loch Creran, while another crucial link was from Port Appin to the island of Lismore.

Such is the area encompassed by the first section of this book, but before taking to the road it is necessary to visit Inverary on Loch Fyne, which has such a prominent place in the history of the Land of Lorn. The long-standing intricacies of clan rivalry, feuds and internecine warfare in western Argyll lie outside the scope of this book; suffice to say, however, at various times in history the power of individual clans, especially that of the MacDougalls and the MacDonalds, waxed and waned. The ultimate victors, acting as a bulwark of royal authority in the west, were the Campbells, created Dukes of Argyll in 1703. Their original home is thought to have been at Innis Chonnel in Loch Awe until the first castle was built at Inverary during the mid-fifteenth century. Inverary on Loch Fyne became the ultimate seat of Campbell power and authority, which eventually spread like an ever-lengthening shadow across the Land of Lorn. But times change, the right of pit and gallows is long gone, and Campbell 'justice' is no longer dispensed from a local courthouse packed with Campbell jurors.

Inverary, c.1900. The town, sometimes known as Half Town, clusters around the spit of land protruding into Loch Fyne. The castle (foreground) is a mid-eighteenth century replacement of the late medieval tower, and an early example of the neo-Scottish Baronial style.

A familiar scene in the early years of the last century: passengers disembark from PS *Lord of the Isles*. Inverary was one of her regular ports of call.

Before either the railway or motor car had penetrated to the head of Loch Awe, the tracks and primitive roads were the preserve of pedlar, horseman and stagecoach. Between Inverary and Oban the post was carried by mail-coach via Dalmally and Taynuilt, both of which had posting establishments catering specifically for the needs of travellers, and change-houses where the toiling horses could be refreshed or replaced in order to keep the mails moving.

These two photographs of Dalmally illustrate the setting ideally. The rivers Lochy, Orchy and Strae, together with numerous streams, drain into the Strath of Orchy at the head of Loch Awe. The broad valley is both gentle and fertile, a complete contrast to mighty Ben Cruachan (3,689 feet) which has seven peaks, spread over a range of 4 miles, and whose overall circumference exceeds 20 miles. The view from the summit is regarded by many as among the finest mountain landscapes in Scotland. The photographs date to c.1905 and 1935 respectively, the latter also showing the line of the Callander and Oban Railway which reached Dalmally from the east in 1877.

H.E. CAMPBELL, MERCHANTS, DALMALLY.

Sizeable settlements in this part of Argyll were few and far between; Inverary lay 15 miles distant, Taynuilt and Oban 14 and 26 miles respectively. At the turn of the twentieth century local merchants such as Campbell's provided essential supplies and served a wide area around the strath. Before the age of mass communication, such shops were also important meeting places to exchange news and gossip.

George W. Daly evidently provided a variety of very different services – watchmaker, jeweller, agent for Pullars Dye Works and purveyor of Cadbury's chocolate. He also sold local view postcards, and several in my collection bear his imprint. Perhaps a reader may know whether Mr Daly himself is shown standing in the doorway of this *c.*1905 picture.

G.W. Daly, Watchmaker & Jeweller, Dalmally. N.B.

Built around 1804 to replace a much older inn and change-house associated with the Glenorchy fairs, the Dalmally Hotel is pictured here in the early years of the twentieth century. One can only speculate about Bruce's Stone, which remains by the roadside. History records his military campaigns either side of Dalmally (in Strathfillan and the Pass of Brander), but whether the future King of Scotland actually sat on the stone, or even mounted his horse from it, we shall never know.

By the seventeenth century the parish of Glenorchy extended from Black Mount in the north to Inishail on Loch Awe, and the present church is believed to be the third built on this island site in the River Orchy. Edinburgh architect James Elliot produced plans in 1808, work went ahead the following year and the church opened for worship in March 1811. The unusual octagonal design resulted in a conical-shaped roof built of fine timbers (said to incorporate the last remnants of the pine forest of nearby Glen Strae) and tiled with Easdale slate. The churchyard contains a number of fourteenth and fifteenth century carved and sculptured slabs of the 'Loch Awe school' (some connected with the MacGregors, who once held sway in this locality), while in a corner an area is known as 'the tinker children's graves'. A travelling family regularly left offerings here on their periodic visits a century ago. The manse was built by John Stevenson of Oban between 1804 and 1805.

Two scenes from around the strath at different seasons. Captioned 'View in Glenorchy with corries of Cruachan', the upper picture is a scene of high summer. The harvest has been gathered in, and the neatly thatched conical hayricks in the stackyard are a sight to behold. By contrast 'The Cottages' at Stronmilichan lie under winter snow; the land is frozen, the cattle will be safely in the byre, and nothing moves. A century ago far greater numbers of people worked the land. Possessing the accumulated knowledge and skills gleaned from a lifetime among the hills, they were in tune with nature, the ever-changing seasons and the annual tasks which needed to be undertaken.

Simple structures of stone with a fireplace let into one or both end walls and a roof of rushes, straw or turf, were once typically home to thousands throughout the Highlands and Islands. The central section usually accommodated a bed, and was flanked by a kitchen and another room. Facilities which we take for granted today were totally absent. By the time of this photograph, c.1900, captioned 'A cottar's house, Dalmally', the Napier Commission hearings had made the Crofters' Holdings Act of 1886 a reality, and the previous injustices suffered by crofters were gradually being remedied by the twin provisions of security of tenure and the fixing of fair rents.

Kilchurn Castle stands on a low, rocky peninsula at the north-eastern extremity of Loch Awe where there was once much clan rivalry. Tradition suggests the site was an early MacGregor stronghold, but the clan subsequently lost it – together with their adjoining lands in Glen Strae and Glen Orchy – to the Campbells. Built and added to between the fifteenth and seventeenth centuries, the earliest surviving section is a five-storey tower-house built by Sir Colin Campbell of Glenorchy, founder of the Breadalbane family, about 1440. Briefly besieged in 1654, but not taken, the castle was garrisoned during both Jacobite rebellions by Hanoverian troops at the invitation of the Campbells. For a period, a castle cellar was used by Loch Awe fishermen as a store for salt and preserved fish. Struck by lightning and unroofed c.1769, the castle rapidly decayed.

By 1880 significant developments around the head of Loch Awe were coming to fruition. The engineers and navvy workforce of the Caledonian and Oban Railway Company had conquered the most difficult section of track around the great granite flank of Ben Cruachan and into the Pass of Brander. Lochawe Station opened on 1 July 1880. On a crag above the station, Duncan Fraser, financially assisted by the Earl of Breadalbane, was building a fine hotel subsequently completed at a cost of about £7,000. This represented an immense leap of faith, as the whole area was virgin territory. Seen here in solitary splendour shortly after completion, the new hotel's windows overlooked Loch Awe and Kilchurn Castle (middle distance).

Lochawe Station, looking west. The Earl also built a pier alongside the new station; access to the platforms was by footbridge, and stone steps led invitingly upwards to the hotel terrace. A lift conveyed luggage to and from the platform – all of which made a very convenient interchange for travellers.

An Oban-bound train at Lochawe Station in the 1920s. Bakery baskets awaiting collection by the signal box had, perhaps, originally brought food for hungry hotel guests!

Loch Awe Hotel, Loch Awe, Argyllshire (Loch Awe Station, Cal. Rly.)
Electric Light   Motor Garage, etc.   Golf Course

An advertising postcard produced for the Loch Awe Hotel, c.1910. By the end of Queen Victoria's reign, a number of luxurious mansions had been built around Loch Awe, and the new station and its pier became significantly busier, especially during the fishing and shooting seasons. Lochawe village grew, and tourist demand led to the hotel being enlarged by the addition of a new wing 'elegantly furnished and fitted up with all the latest improvements'. Electric lighting was installed. A winter garden and a large smoking room overlooking the loch were added. Salmon and trout fishing could be enjoyed free of charge. Lawn tennis, croquet, boating, billiards and carriages were available – and guides were provided for ascents of Ben Cruachan. To meet the needs of the new age of motoring a garage was available for guests' vehicles.

The SS *Countess of Breadalbane* was the first of several vessels purchased by the hotel, and she operated for over 50 years until the mid-1930s. She made special morning trips to view the Falls of Cruachan, and sailed the 24

CHEAP DAY TRIPS FROM ALL CALEDONIAN RAILWAY STATIONS

LUNCH TEA &c. SERVED ON BOARD.

DUNCAN FRASER PROPRIETOR.

SALOON STEAMER "COUNTESS OF BREADALBANE" ON LOCHAWE.

mile length of Loch Awe to Ford. For tourists it was the golden age of the daily round trip, and all manner of ingenious itineraries were available via Loch Awe. The combined use of rail, coach and steamer travel brought Glen Nant, Oban and the Pass of Melfort, Black Mount, Inverary (to connect with PS *Lord of the Isles*), Iona and Staffa within the reach of all.

ST. CONANS KIRK, LOCH AWE.   89319. J.V.

EAST AISLE, ST CONANS CHURCH, LOCH AWE   AB423

St Conan, the patron saint of Lorn, was a disciple of St Columba. Several nearby locations are associated with his life – Glen Orchy, Dalmally and Innis Chonain in Loch Awe, his reputed burial-place. Walter Douglas Campbell (architect, woodcarver and collector) of Innis Chonain, his sister, and finally their trustees, were responsible for the building and furnishing of this church at Lochawe between 1881 and 1930. Boulders of Cruachan granite were rolled down the mountainside to be split and shaped on site. The circumstances of its building, in this unrivalled setting overlooking Loch Awe, the superb craftsmanship throughout and the incorporation of disparate architectural styles all combine to make a visit to this church an absolutely unique experience. That it happened at all was apparently due to Campbell's elderly mother who found the long drive to Dalmally church too difficult, so he built her one nearer home!

Post Office, Loch Awe.

This postcard bears the Lochawe cancellation and was mailed from this very post office on 6 June 1913. The passing car displays an original Argyllshire registration plate.

The gigantic forces of glaciation once at work in the lands of Lorn produced the 24 mile slash across the Argyll landscape between Dalmally and Ford which we know today as Loch Awe. In the Highlands, history, legend, folklore and myth often become entwined, and unsurprisingly there are several primaeval legends concerning the creation of this loch. While details vary, the main aspects are often remarkably similar:

The floor of this great loch was once a fertile valley where harvest fields were rich with grain, and where sheep and cattle grazed. In a corrie high up on Cruachan there was a spring of water which according to faery command was always kept covered by a slab of stone. But the folk of the valley grew careless, and a girl forgot to replace the capstone after drawing water at sunset. All night long the water cascaded down the slopes of Cruachan with the result that by morning the valley below had become a vast sheet of water studded with islands.

Footnote:
Strictly speaking, mid-twentieth century developments fall outside the remit of this book, but before moving on I feel compelled to mention the staggering engineering achievement completed in the 1960s whereby Ben Cruachan was given an electrical heart to produce electricity for the national grid. A visitor centre lies at the entrance to the Pass of Brander, and those interested should view the static displays and take the short bus ride into 'the hollow mountain' to see the generator sets in the vast turbine hall. This area was cut from solid rock, is big enough to absorb Coventry Cathedral without difficulty, and is located 118 feet below the normal level of Loch Awe.

By general consent, the Pass of Brander (or Pass of Awe) is melancholy, gloomy and intimidating – a place from which the sun is excluded for most of the year. Photographs are often unsatisfactory and rarely do the feature justice; instead a chromolithograph of 1893 is reproduced here. On the eastern side, both road and railway squeeze between Loch Awe and the towering crags of Cruachan, while just 100 yards across the loch, the sheer cliffs of Creag an Aoineadh plunge 900 feet to the water. Cattle were once driven this way from the lands of the west to the great trysts at Crieff and Falkirk. Also known as Am Brannraidh ('Place of Ambush'), the Pass was of great importance in the days of the clans and witnessed many skirmishes and at least two major battles, those being in 1297 and 1308. In the latter, King Robert Bruce obtained his revenge for his own defeat two years earlier at Dalrigh in Strathfillan by ambushing and completely routing a large force of MacDougalls led by John of Lorn which was cut to pieces.

The three-arched stone Bridge of Awe was completed in 1779, but as Haldane speculates in his authoritative work, *The Drove Roads of Scotland*, it may not have been the first bridge on this site. Sadly the old structure shown in this pre-First World War photograph was swept away by a huge volume of water in January 1992; only short sections of the once important crossing now remain either side of the Awe. These lie a short way upstream of the more modern bridge, which carries the main road to Oban, built in 1937/1938.

Right: Beyond the Pass, the road originally followed the eastern bank of the Awe, past Inverawe House set in a well-wooded landscape, continuing down to the river-mouth at Bonawe on the southern shore of Loch Etive. This house, with its crow-stepped gables, has been a seat of the Campbells of Inverawe since the sixteenth century, although the present structure dates mainly from the nineteenth century with later alterations made by Sir Robert Lorimer. Tales of ghostly happenings are recited in these parts; mention the name Ticonderoga and you will hear a very strange story indeed.

Centre and below: Bonawe or Bun Atha ('Mouth of the Awe') was a historic ferrying-place not only over the river for Taynuilt (known locally as the 'Penny Ferry'), but also across Loch Etive where the ferry once formed the principal connection with the land route between North Lorn and beyond, and the Pass of Brander. These photographs date from the 1920s; the ferry has long since ceased, and the ferryman's cottage is no more.

A Good Days Catch on River Awe - a 52 pounder.

A more gentle, open landscape greets the traveller around the shores of Loch Etive, and after crossing the River Awe, Taynuilt village is reached. Writing in 1934, that well-respected Highlander, the late Seton Gordon (author, photographer and naturalist), believed the average size of Awe salmon to be unequalled in British rivers, and he cites an angler catching two salmon of some 56 lbs weight in different years. The specimen of 52 lbs proudly displayed here (c.1915) is not exactly unimpressive either.

The point of interest in this c.1909 picture is not the Taynuilt Temperance Hotel, but the standing stone on the hill known as Cnoc Aingeal ('Hill of Sacrificial Fires'), also visible in the previous photograph. Prior to 1805 this monolith of grey granite, measuring 16 feet in length and weighing 4 tons, lay in a field about a mile to the west. During that year, the year of the naval engagement at Trafalgar, workmen from the Lorn Iron Furnace dragged the stone on rollers to this spot and raised it as a memorial to Lord Nelson. It was the first such monument to our naval hero in the British Isles, predating the national monument in Trafalgar Square by 37 years. The forthcoming section on the Lorn Furnace will explain why Taynuilt has this distinction.

A thatcher at work in Taynuilt village, *c*.1898. While methods of thatching differ throughout the British Isles according to local tradition and custom, such skilled workers were always in demand in an age when far greater numbers of buildings were roofed with either reed, ling, rush, bavin or turf.

Villagers and employees of both Campbell's Stores and the Argyle Stores watch the photographer at work as he 'clicks' the camera shutter to record this scene in Main Street, *c*.1909.

In this 1931 photograph, Main Street has a tarmacadam surface more suited to the motoring age, and appropriate services are now available at the garage (centre, right).

A young man who had himself served in the Great War attended the unveiling of the war memorial to take this photograph on 24 November 1921. He had only recently left the Navy to settle in Oban and establish his own photographic business. On the reverse, the picture carries the imprint: 'H. M. Scrivens, Photographic Artist, Oban', and is in consequence one of his earliest photographs.

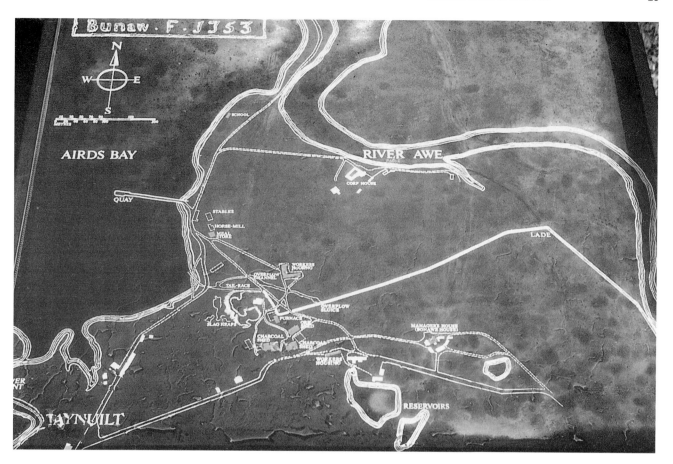

The Lorn Furnace was established by Cumbrian ironmasters in 1752/1753 on the southern shore of Loch Etive between the Rivers Nant and Awe. For some 120 years smelting took place there, giving employment to up to 600 men at any one time. Local landowners Sir Duncan Campbell of Lochnell and the Earl of Breadalbane entered into agreements with the company for both the site and the cutting of woodland (see title page). The surrounding hills were rich in woods of alder, ash, birch, hazel and oak, and timber-gathering operations ultimately extended over 34 square miles around the shores of Loch Etive and into Glen Nant. A range of industrial buildings was worked into the contours of the land in such a way as to aid the movement of large amounts of material. Iron ore was brought by sailing ship from Cumberland up Loch Etive to Kelly's Pier in Airds Bay, unloaded and taken by horse and cart up to the ore shed. Charcoal collected from kilns all around the locality was bagged and transported to two large sheds located on a slope above the charging-house, the heart of the whole operation.

Essential to the process of iron-smelting were iron ore, charcoal and limestone flux. A proportionately exact mix of material heated to high temperatures produced molten iron which could then be drawn off. Water was diverted from the River Awe and an iron waterwheel provided motive power for two large pairs of bellows, thus ensuring a continuous blast to the furnace. From the nearby quay, the end products of pig iron and round shot (cannonballs) weighing from 3 to 32 lbs were shipped back to Furness. Cannonballs manufactured in Taynuilt were used by the British Navy at the time of Lord Nelson's stunning victories, thereby establishing a link between this little-known Highland community and one of our national heroes. The furnace community was virtually self-supporting, having workers' accommodation on site together with farmhouses, a meal store, stables, laundry, bakery, church, hall – and an inn. At one time both drunkenness and smuggling were rife. Historic Scotland has done a splendid job in preserving a remarkably complete range of early industrial buildings, and in waymarking and interpreting the site. The author's photograph of their plan of the area (above) will enable all the main features to be identified.

Top: The charging-house: charcoal and iron ore were 'barrowed' along slate tracks from nearby sheds through the open doorway (left) to begin the iron-making process.

Above: Anticlockwise from the casting-house (right), site of blowing-house (behind fence nearest camera), smithy and store (left, centre). The sunken channel among the trees (top, left) took the tailrace into Loch Etive. (Photographs taken by the author, 1999.)

Somewhat confusingly, the district around the quarries visible across Loch Etive from Taynuilt, is also known as Bonawe. This ancient stone jetty on the northern side of the loch was once the main crossing place in the whole area for those travelling routes north or south. Loch Etive is an immense sea-loch, the head of which lies 10 miles distant towards the mountains of Glen Coe, away to the north-east (left, in this 1880s photograph).

At the same spot but some 40 years later, Henry Scrivens, watched by several children, captured this scene on film. It is as well he did for the ferryman's house is now but a memory, having been demolished to make way for an altogether quite different house.

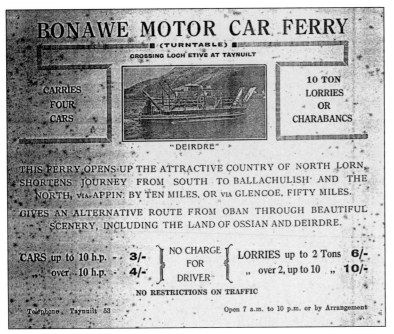

A vehicular ferry eventually replaced the small rowing boat of earlier years. Foot passengers were also carried, including workmen who lived in Taynuilt, but worked by day in the Bonawe quarries. Fortunately this interesting handbill, the paper foxed by ageing, has survived in the quarry office. The shortened journey times and appropriate charges for various classes of vehicles are detailed for this new service to motorists in the 1930s. (My thanks to John Martin of Bonawe who kindly provided a copy of this poster.)

The ferry died a death in stages as the labour requirement in the quarries diminished, and the newly built Connel Ferry Bridge further downstream became the primary crossing. Vehicles ceased to be carried towards the end of the Second World War, but foot passenger traffic continued into the 1950s. The jetty which had seen so much activity, and the exchange of conversation and news from afar, now lies gently decaying. This view across the still waters of the loch towards Taynuilt was taken by the author in 1988. For me, the neglected, abandoned pier now has a sad atmosphere; time to move on . . .

In the 1880s, J. & A. Gardner and Co. began quarrying granite where the rocky outcrops of Ben Duirinnis (1,821 feet) descend steeply to the waters of Loch Etive at Bonawe. Vast quantities of granite setts for road paving, masonry blocks and even curling stones were produced here until 1945. Each sett-maker or mason had his own hut by the lochside. Stone was supplied to the working area from the quarry face by means of a light tramway, which was also used to transport the finished product to the deep-water quay for loading and shipping. Other workers employed included labourers, carters, blacksmiths, drillers and blasters – the latter bringing down sometimes huge amounts of rock using copious amounts of gunpowder.

Mailed from the Quarries Post Office in 1910, this postcard shows the SS *Bonawe* loading stone. In 1929 a Dr Bernard H. Knight produced a technical paper concerning the suitability of various types of granite for roadmaking, and his conclusions put beyond doubt what everyone locally knew already – Bonawe stone was best! Quite simply, being so hard, it never wore out. Granite setts fashioned here paved many streets in Greenock, Paisley and Glasgow (e.g. Miller Street, West George Street (1907) and the King George V Bridge (1928)). Further afield, both the floor and entrances to the Mersey Tunnel were constructed using Bonawe stone.

To (Name of Company), *Messrs. J. & A. Gardner, Glasgow.*

(1) I hereby agree that while I am in your employment you shall deduct from the wages to be earned by me the amount of my house rent (should I occupy any house of which you are the owners or lessees), the sums from time to time to be paid by you on my behalf for medicine and medical attendance, the price of fuel supplied by you to me and payments due by me to you in respect of the use of materials, tools or machines, light or heat, or in respect of any other thing to be done or provided by you in relation to my work.

(2) Should I think fit to have my tools sharpened or repaired by you, I agree that you should deduct the charges therefor from my wages.

(3) I request you, until I give you notice in writing to the contrary, to pay on my behalf :—

    (*a*) Occupiers' rates on any house occupied by me ;

    (*b*) Contributions to Welfare Schemes, Workmen's Institutes, Hospitals, charitable and other objects usually contributed to at the Colliery.

(4) Should I occupy any house belonging to or leased by you, such occupancy shall continue only during my employment with you, and shall be terminable at any time on one week's notice.

(5) I acknowledge that I have received a copy of this Agreement.

M'Naughtan & Sinclair, Printers, Glasgow.

In the 1920s, quarry workers were required to sign their agreement to these conditions of employment.

A rare picture showing the inside of a sett-maker's hut, *c*.1920. 'Good stone' split easily along a well-defined grain enabling those on piece-work to earn 12/- per ton of prepared setts. 'Bad stone' had irregular graining, was difficult to work, and resulted in a smaller pay-packet. (Photograph reproduced here by kind permission of John Martin.)

The sett-makers' and masons' working bank.

The workforce reached a peak of about 330 before the First World War, but with the inclusion of their family members the Bonawe community could boast a population of some 1,000 persons. Sons followed fathers into the quarry; it was a way of life.

The original settlement, which lay along the lochside further to the east beyond the present quarry, was replaced about 1911 by terraced houses and tenement blocks. These later buildings are now ruinous, where they exist at all. Always a close-knit community, Bonawe was largely self-supporting, having a laundry, bakery, shop, post office, schools, community hall and billiard room.

John's Point, The Gullet and The Ramparts were among the many names given to the living quarters. While walking here in 1988 to take this photograph of an abandoned block, a local resident told me that it had been known as Fairy Island. Today, just five men work the quarry producing crushed granite for modern road construction.

Priors, Ardchattan, Benderloch.

Ardchattan Priory was founded by Duncan MacDougall of Lorn in 1230, and was one of only three houses of the Valliscaulian order in Scotland, the others being Pluscarden in Moray and Beauly. The order adopted Cistercian practices, was limited to 20 in number (including lay-brothers) and was dependent on its mother-house, Val des Choux in Burgundy. Following the Reformation the priory fell into disuse, and part of the buildings were converted into a private dwelling-house. Significant ruins still survive, together with an important collection of late medieval graveslabs and carved stones.

9985   SELMA AND LOWER KEIL, BENDERLOCH.

Two miles beyond the priory, the old road to Benderloch keeps closely to the lochside, passing the eighteenth century church at Ardchattan. From the lands to the north of Ben Lora, pall-bearers once carried their dead by an ancient coffin route, around the slopes of Ben Lora, for interment here. Port Selma, which lies on the far side of this mountain, was once a place of importance and 100 years ago perhaps a dozen boats would have been drawn up on the pebbly shore of Ardmucknish Bay in front of these former ferrymens' cottages. Before the opening of the Ballachulish railway line and the road over the Moss of Achnacree, the natural lanes of communication were by sea, and goods were traded between Port Selma, Oban and Port Appin. At one time northbound travellers on foot could make use of a network of smaller ferries – there were several across Loch Creran (including that between South and North Shian), and another from Port Appin to Lismore – right up to the Ballachulish narrows.

Before the Connel to Ballachulish railway was built, this whole coast was a somewhat remote backwater. The scattered population was dependent on the fruits of labour on land and sea, and for the most part Gaelic was spoken. The pace of development quickened in the early years of the last century, and the church, dedicated to St Modan, was built in 1905. The railway had arrived two years previously, and constructional scars on the landscape are all too evident in this photograph of *c*.1906. New Selma, which later became more widely known as Benderloch (also the name of the district), was now really on the map.

The mild, moist climate of the west combines with rich soil to give prolific growing conditions, as seen in this garden of abundance opposite St Modan's Church, *c*.1910.

An ancient seat of Pictish royalty, a site used by swordsmiths, and associations with Fingalian legend are all claims made for Beregonium, a vast outcrop of rock surmounted by remnants of a vitrified hill fort. That historically it has been a place of some significance is without doubt.

The smithy, Benderloch, *c*.1905. Repairer of agricultural implements, wheelwright and shoer of horses – the blacksmith was a lynchpin in the rural economy at this time. The smithy, which saw much activity, still stands, but scenes such as this have passed into history.

John Campbell (1823–1897) the Ledaig Bard and Bard of Clan Campbell, was a Gaelic writer and poet whose collected works were published in both Gaelic and English in Edinburgh (1884). He was also postmaster at Ledaig Post Office, and a naturalist and botanist whose garden produce was taken to Oban for sale. In addition he taught Sunday school in a cave chapel by the shore. Former pupils and friends worldwide raised funds for his memorial, the hall (in the distance at the bend in the road), but this is now Campbell Hall Cottage, and the original stained glass window there has been removed to the church.

The branch railway line between Connel and Ballachulish opened on 24 August 1903. Throughout the 28 mile length and 70 minute journey time, passengers could experience continuous views of the sea and scenes of stunning beauty as the train wound its way up the coast. The excessively large station buildings and signal boxes that characterised this line could never have been justified. Dr Beeching swung his axe in 1966 and the rest is history. Like much in this book, Benderloch Station, seen here *c*.1905, has vanished. But stand on the site today, and the view towards Craigneuk, the distinctive rocky outcrop of Ben Lora which overhangs the road at Ledaig, remains the same.

Black's Stores, *c*.1905. Angus Black, who also had a shop in Connel, had a sharp eye for business, and on the building of the railway he lost no time in establishing his new store opposite Benderloch Station. Nowadays the shop is known as Munro's Stores, being run by Campbell Munro. By a neat twist of fate it also incorporates the older post office business from nearby Ledaig which his great-grandfather, the Bard, had operated in the nineteenth century.

LOCH NELL TOWER,
BENDERLOCH

Lochnell Castle (*c.*1900) is set among woods at the head of Ardmucknish Bay opposite Benderloch. The family most closely associated with this house is that of Campbell of Lochnell, whose founder, John, second son of Colin, 3rd Earl of Argyll, is recorded as being laird here in 1536. At one time the estate extended to Taynuilt. The building, which incorporates work ranging in date from the late seventeenth to early nineteenth centuries, has survived several disastrous fires, most notably that of 1853 which largely gutted the property. The family line has produced several distinguished military men, including Sir Duncan Campbell, a founder of the Black Watch.

Lady Margaret's Tower is inscribed 'Erected by Lady Campbell, Anno. 1754'. She was the second wife of Sir Duncan Campbell, 7th of Lochnell. Legend has it that Lady Margaret, a Cameron, had the castellated-style tower built in what transpired to be a forlorn hope of being able to glimpse the Lochaber hills of her childhood home. Nevertheless, the outlook tower, which is sited on an elevated ridge in the castle grounds, provides magnificent prospects of Loch Linnhe, Loch Etive and Mull.

Eriska, 3½ miles from Benderloch Station.   Photo. by D. Mackay, Bookseller, Oban.

North-west of Benderloch, byroads intersect near Barcaldine Castle. One heads towards the former jetty and ferry-house at South Shian, while the other becomes a private road which crosses the tidal channel of An Doirlinn by a bridge into the policies of Eriska. A crannog, partially excavated in 1884, is indicative of habitation over 2,000 years ago, while ecclesiastical ownership in the fifteenth and sixteenth centuries suggests that Eriska may have been an island sanctuary. The 'big house' was built in 1884 by a branch of the Stewarts of Appin, but James Melis Stuart, the original owner, barely survived its completion. The architect, Hippolyte Blanc, was renowned for demanding the most exacting specifications. Blocks of sandstone and grey granite were reputedly brought up to the site from the jetty by means of a light tramway, and in later years coal delivered by puffer into the bay was similarly transported to heat the extensive hothouses, which produced peaches, nectarines and grapes. A luxurious country house hotel today, Eriska, owned by the Buchanan-Smith family, welcomes returning guests year after year who come to refresh body and spirit.

Barcaldine Castle, built between 1594 and 1609 by Sir Duncan Campbell ('Black Duncan') of Glenorchy (1546–1631), was one of a network of seven fortifications built to protect the extensive Campbell lands. Like all chiefs of his time, Sir Duncan had the power of life or death in his hands; the site of the notorious Hanging Knowe (Tom a chrochaidh) lies but a short distance from the castle door. During its period of abandonment and ruin in the nineteenth century, travelling tinkers occasionally found shelter within the nine-foot thick walls. Shown here roofless c.1895, the fortified tower underwent a comprehensive programme of restoration between 1897 and 1911. The histories of the castle and the various branches of Clan Campbell are well displayed, and the discerning visitor will find much of interest.

In years past at Rubha Garbh, 1½ miles north-east of the castle, a rowing boat ferried travellers over Loch Creran between Benderloch and the lands of Appin. Two miles further along the lochside lies the 'big house', built by Para Djarak Campbell, 4th of Balcardine, for his family in 1709. The house at Innerergan was known at one time as Dalfure, and nowadays as Barcaldine House (seen here c.1903). One of Campbell's extravagant successors incurred overwhelming debt by adding shrubberies, specimen trees, orchards and a 3-acre 20-foot high walled garden, complete with heated glasshouses producing nectarines, peaches, pineapples and other exotica. All these excesses resulted in the enforced disposal of the estate in 1842. The house has since had a chequered history, and currently provides holiday accommodation.

Creagan Bridge, 1904. Following the closure of the Ballachulish branch railway line in 1966, the magnificent views from this bridge had been experienced only by walkers. The graceful lines of the two girder spans and the distinctive masonry arches had been a familiar part of the Loch Creran landscape since they were put in place by the Arrol Bridge Company in 1903. This well-known landmark was dismantled and replaced by a road bridge in mid-1999. The expenditure of £3 million has resulted in motorists no longer having to make the 5½ mile circuit around the head of the loch, where occasional high tides flooded the road, causing a diversion through private property.

Creagan Inn, 1904. The inn, which lies close to another historic ferrying-place across Loch Creran, is a very ancient hostelry. 'The lintel of Creagan Inn was so low in the old days that even I had to stoop; and the double-hinged door was so narrow that the second half had to be opened to admit an ordinary man. Add to all this the fact that the landlady was so deaf that a request for refreshment had to be bawled in such a stentorian voice that anyone across the loch could tell what you were having' (*The Land of Lorne* by T. Ratcliffe Barnett, 1933).

Appin is the land of the Stewarts, and the scene of a cause célèbre, 'the Appin murder'. The essentials were that a Campbell was shot and a Stewart was convicted on the flimsiest of evidence by a Campbell jury at Inverary. Every account I have read suggests that the wrong man was hung at Ballachulish, and although it all happened 250 years ago, the events left a lasting impression on the district as profound as the massacre of Glen Coe. At Tynribbie, pictured here, a road from Port Appin (which lies 2 miles distant) joins the primary route through the Strath of Appin.

Portnacroish ('Haven of the Cross'), Appin, 1904.

APPIN HOTEL,
APPIN,
ARGYLL.

TELEPHONE No. 29.
TELEGRAMS: "HOTEL, APPIN."

Appin Hotel advertising stationery.

Appin Hotel and Castle Stalker, 1904. In the early twentieth century, many happy holidays in Appin and district started at this popular hotel, which enjoyed an elevated position overlooking Loch Laich and the ruined castle. For those without their own transport, its proximity to Appin railway station was an advantage, a fact that no doubt led to the adoption of the name Station Hotel for a time in later years. Sadly, a fire destroyed the building *c*. World War Two.

The origins of Castle Stalker (Eilean an Stalcaire), the 'Castle of the Falconer', are thought to date from the thirteenth century. In 1320 it was owned by Sir John Stewart of Lorne, and repaired about 1450 as a hunting seat by Duncan Stewart of Appin, seneschal to his kinsman King James IV. Perched on a rocky islet in Loch Laich about 200 yards from the shore, the castle, which commands views of Loch Linnhe and the Strath, consists of a rectangular keep, the entrance door to which is at first floor level. Hanoverian troops were garrisoned here in the 'Forty-five', but in the early nineteenth century the castle fell into a ruinous state. This persisted until the mid-1960s when an extensive scheme of reconstruction returned the property to a private dwelling. In this photograph of *c*.1905 several people are seated on the greensward under the castle walls, while another group can be seen on the shore.

The shallow inner saltings around the head of Loch Laich were crossed barefoot by the travellers of old; the fording-place was marked by two large stakes. Tourists today reach Port Appin (illustrated here) by road from Tynribbie. The nucleus of the oldest settlement clusters on the bay close to the old pier, amid a landscape of glen, mountain, islands and extensive sea views, all of which make a stunning combination of scenery so typical of the whole coast between Connel and Ballachulish.

A map of 1747 marks 'Ferry Inn' where Airds Hotel now stands. Cattle from the island of Lismore were once brought across by boat and driven this way to the mainland trysts. The sender of this postcard was at the hotel on 5 July 1907 'having a very happy time'. Happy times continue as, for a number of years, the Allen family have established a very considerable reputation for cuisine and creature comforts here.

The 'big house' of Airds is a striking early Georgian property overlooking Airds Bay to Lismore and the mountains of Mull and Morvern. The central section of the main block rises to a triangular pediment, the tympanum of which displays the full armorial achievement of the Campbells of Airds in bold relief. The motto is 'Be Mindfull'.

Port Appin Pier

Small and often remote piers such as this had an importance which nowadays in an age of instant communication is often difficult to grasp. Goods of every conceivable description would be unloaded here for delivery by horse and cart to the scattered population of the district. Periodically ships brought tourists and also news from afar, and it would not have been unusual for news of, say, Queen Victoria's death in 1901, to have been received several days after the event in such isolated communities.

The ship at the distant pierhead c.1910 would appear to have the lines of PS *Fusilier*. Records of the local ferry which connected with the island of Lismore (left) date back to as early as c.1630. Pier House, the old ferry-house (foreground), consists of a pair of early nineteenth century cottages built parallel to each other and constructed of lime-washed rubble with slate roofs and bowed gable ends on the shore side. The space between the two was formerly roofed over to form a boathouse, but is now incorporated into the overall building, as shown in the photograph below, taken by the author in 1982.

Anchored like a ship in Loch Linnhe, the low, green fertile island of Lismore (the 'Great Garden') is 9 miles in length and about 1 mile wide; the highest point is Barr Mór (417 feet). Surprisingly, there is much to see on this island which St Moluag, a contemporary of St Columba, made a centre for his missionary work in the sixth century. This brief mention of Lismore, glimpsed across the water from Port Appin, brings this section to a close.

OBAN – GLEN NANT – FORD

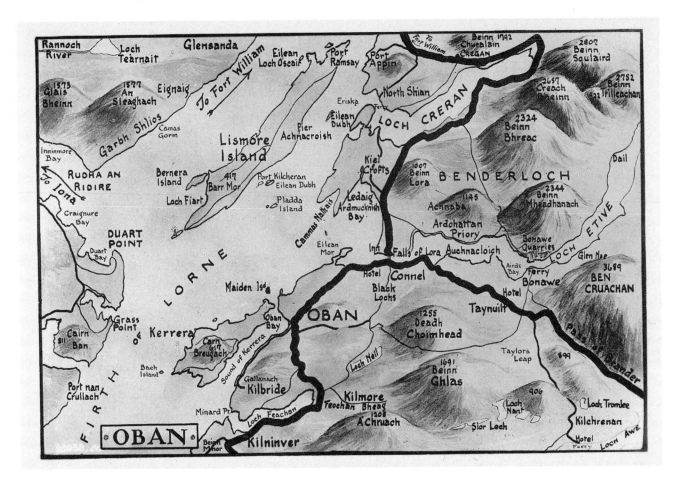

The name Oban is of Gaelic origin, being derived from *òb* (a bay) and the diminutive particle *an* ('the little bay'). The anchorage on the south side of this bay is generally referred to as being the oldest.

Several significant archaeological discoveries dating from 1869 prove that the area occupied by present-day Oban (together with some of the outlying islands) was settled by Mesolithic man about 6500 BC. These nomadic hunter-gatherers lived in caves, and fashioned antler and bone into barbed heads for their fish-spears. In more recent times the most important factor in the town's development has been its geographical location around the bay, which provides such a superb natural asset. The low green island of Kerrera lies in the Firth of Lorn athwart Oban Bay, and the sea lanes either side of the island give access to the crescent-shaped anchorage which the town overlooks.

By the seventeenth century the bay offered shelter to Atlantic herring fishermen, and in the first quarter of the following century, a Renfrew company established a trading station. Development was further stimulated by the building of a customs house at the far end of Shore Street in 1760, and subsequently by the enterprise of the brothers Hugh and John Stevenson who were extensively engaged in business as general merchants, having trading sloops plying regularly between Oban and Glasgow, Liverpool and Irish ports. They also established a shipbuilding yard and a distillery, and were widely employed as stonemasons, being responsible for much building in the town, particularly around George Street, Tweeddale Street, Stafford Street and Argyll Street. As a consequence of their substantial accomplishments it is hardly surprising that they are regarded as being the town's founding fathers.

In 1812, Henry Bell's pioneering engineering achievement *The Comet* – the first commercially successful steamboat in Europe – began operating a regular service between Glasgow and Oban. Such a landmark development gave a spur to the construction of the town's earliest harbour buildings, the South Pier and the adjacent Piermaster's House (*c.*1814). The western sea lanes became increasingly busy with both trade and tourism following the opening of the Crinan and Caledonian Canals, which provided a through route to the Highland capital, Inverness. Such commercial developments were responsible for the increase in Oban's population which grew from 586 in 1791 to 1,398 by 1841. Under the Reform Act of 1832 the status of the town was further enhanced by achieving parliamentary burgh status.

During the eighteenth century several notable travellers came to the area, among them Thomas Pennant, Mrs Grant of Laggan, and Johnson and Boswell who left accounts or references of their experiences. Between 1800 and 1850 Oban seemed rarely out of the news as international figures of the day 'discovered' the Highlands and Islands, with the result that visits by writers, musicians, artists and royalty became almost commonplace. Among these were Sir Walter Scott (1814); Felix Mendelssohn to compose his Fingal's Cave (or Hebrides) Overture (1829); J. M. W. Turner, the renowned artist (1830); William and Dorothy Wordsworth (1833); and King George of Saxony (1844). Above all, it was the visit by Queen Victoria and Prince Albert in 1847 that put the ultimate seal of approval to cruising in West Highland waters; the itinerary they had taken was known thereafter as 'The Royal Route'.

Two further significant happenings would have a profound effect on the growth of Oban. As a result of various amalgamations of Glasgow-based shipping interests, the name of MacBrayne has been synonymous with the Highlands and Islands since 1879; to step aboard a MacBrayne steamer would provide a gateway to an intricate network of tours and excursions to mainland and island destinations along the length of the Scottish west coast from Glasgow to that remotest of all outposts, St Kilda. 'The islands are Oban's distant suburbs, and the town – linked by a constant passage of the red-funnelled steamers – has the unmistakable ambience of the Gaelic west', wrote one commentator. Secondly, the arrival of the railway in 1880 (of which more later) brought a variety of destinations north of Glasgow and Edinburgh within reach of London. Those intending to travel from the south, bound for what many thought to be 'the back of beyond', might have been comforted by seeing Oban described as 'The Charing Cross of the Highlands' in that little red pocket guide for tourists published by Ward, Lock & Co. in 1897. By the end of the nineteenth century, the explosive growth fuelled by tourism had transformed Oban from the 'small straggling village' of 1800 into the thriving economic and social capital of Lorn.

For those interested in a detailed history of Oban, several sources are available. These selective notes on the development of the town up to the 1880s when the ensuing photographs commence may assist the general reader in giving both context and background to the pictures which follow. This section also includes Connel, Glen Nant and Ford, at the southern extremity of Loch Awe.

The town's unofficial pre-1901 insignia which had never received the approval of the Lord Lyon.

The coat of arms incorporates a lion rampant, a gyrony of eight (a Campbell device) and the Galley of Lorn with a blazing cresset at the masthead. The design was approved by the Lord Lyon including the Gaelic wording *AIR ADHART* ('Forward'). The version illustrated was produced for the burgeoning tourist trade, and appears on a postcard of 1904 alongside a general view of the town.

Describing another west coast location, the late Gavin Maxwell immortalised the phrase 'ring of bright water', the words becoming the title of his best-selling book. Such a description might equally be applied to Oban Bay, and these two photographs from differing perspectives taken approximately 30 years apart help to put the town into context with its immediate surroundings. *Above:* the island of Kerrera lies westwards across the bay from Oban with the mountains of Mull and Morvern in the background of this *c.*1900 picture. *Below:* Henry Scrivens' photograph shows the cluster of buildings around the North Pier, the white frontage of the Great Western Hotel (left), and the road leading over the hill to Connel. Nearer the camera, shop sun blinds are visible along George Street, with the gaunt Oban Distillery buildings behind.

These pictures show just a few of the many steamers which became such familiar sights in Oban Bay from the closing years of the nineteenth century and into the next. Built in 1867, PS *Gael* originally undertook the Clyde sailings to Campbeltown. On coming under the MacBrayne flag in 1891, she regularly carried passengers and mail between many mainland and island destinations from Oban to Gairloch, and occasionally as far north as Lochinver. Her long career ended in 1924 when she was scrapped.

The SS *Claymore*, by general consent a beautifully proportioned ship, served the Scottish west coast all year round between 1881 and 1931. Her route was Glasgow to Stornoway, and while she carried tourists in the summer months, it was her cargo and livestock capacity that made her a lifeline to so many small, remote communities more easily reached by sea than overland. (See her also at Diabaig and Gairloch in *Old Ways Through Wester Ross*.)

S.S. Claymore, Oban

'This is a view of the "Chieftain". We saw her come in this afternoon and then leave for Glasgow 2 hours later' (written from the Columba Hotel, Oban on 29 August 1913). Launched in 1907, the *Chieftain* displaced 1,000 tons gross, and although another aesthetic triumph of ship design, she was costly to run and her performance somewhat disappointing so that MacBraynes disposed of her in 1919.

S.S. "Chieftain," Oban

SS *Cygnet* was launched in 1904, and in her early years ran cargo between Glasgow and Inverary, but after the Great War she was based at Oban (seen here at the Railway Pier). Until 1930 *Cygnet* was engaged on the islands' mail services, but was broken up in 1931.

Launched in 1885, PS *Grenadier* became closely associated over many years with the Staffa and Iona route from Oban, and the Ardrishaig winter service from Greenock. During the Great War she was employed on mine-sweeping duties in the North Sea under the name of HMS *Grenade* – the only MacBrayne paddle steamer utilised on active war service. In circumstances never satisfactorily explained, she caught fire in the middle of the night while alongside the North Pier in September 1927, the accident claiming the lives of the long-serving Captain McArthur and two of his crew. When daylight came, Henry Scrivens was on hand to record the sad scene with his camera, his photographs subsequently appearing in the national press.

The Royal Highland Yacht Club was formed in 1881. Its annual regatta took place among a programme of social events, including fashionable balls and the Oban Games, which constituted the Argyllshire Gathering held in the second week of September. A special feature of 'the season' in Oban, it was a time for seeing and above all, *being* seen; the various functions were 'attended by the crème de la crème, not only of Argyllshire society, but of a much wider area'. At such times, onlookers would take much interest in identifying personalities among the comings and goings between the be-flagged yachts – perhaps numbering up to 50 moored in the bay – and the shore. (Photograph reproduced here by kind permission of Robert McCulloch.)

For many Highland estate owners the possession of a steam yacht was an essential adjunct to the 'big house'. Lord Macdonald, whose seat was at Armadale on Skye, Sir Donald Currie (Scalpay), Sir George Bullough (Rum) and the laird of Ardnamurchan, Charles Rudd, to name but four, all possessed them. Indeed, at a time when roads were poor, Rudd's vessel was frequently used for shopping trips, becoming a familiar sight in Oban Bay. In 1914 many such yachts went south, undertaking war service as auxiliaries. In the Depression following the Great War, expensive to crew and operate, those that had survived never regained their former status of earlier years; a way of life had passed into history.

Above: Four hundred navvies were employed constructing the final section of track to Oban. At night the glare of floodlights lit up the sky as they worked around the clock in Glen Cruitten. There was much debate concerning the exact positioning of the new station, one faction even pressing for it to be sited at the North Pier steamer terminal, which would have had the effect of cutting off the town from the sea. In the event, the new Railway Pier was built on recently reclaimed land, with the station alongside (right), and the inaugural banquet was held on the platforms under the huge glazed roof on 30 June 1880.

Below: By the time this *c.*1900 picture was taken, about 20 years had elapsed since the arrival of the railway, and sharp-eyed readers are invited to make a comparison with the upper photograph. In the hills (extreme right), the Hydropathic – of which more later – had already been abandoned.

In his classic Highland work *A Summer in Skye*, published in 1865, Alexander Smith left some enduring observations about the transitory nature of Oban tourism in the mid-Victorian age. But there was no Oban railway in Smith's day – that came later – and times change. In this picture elegant Edwardians arriving by train would be accosted by porters accompanied by their luggage barrows and . . .

. . . liveried coachmen waited to whisk travellers to one of the many hotels and boarding houses. Holidaymakers might now come for a week or two, or perhaps a month at a time, the more wealthy even being accompanied by some of their personal domestic staff.

Alas now but a memory, the original Oban station buildings, incorporating a graceful clock tower crowned by a small spire, were demolished in the mid-1980s. This private photograph showing the station exterior in Argyll Square is dated May 1934.

Top: Oban Station *c.*1905. Advertisement hoardings, hanging gas lamps and a profusion of plants adorn platforms 3, 4 & 5 under the ornate roof. A small group contemplate the fate of two stags'-heads on the platform, trophies no doubt of some sportsman's recent visit to a Highland estate.

Above: First and second generation 'Oban Bogies' (left and right respectively), the latter designed for greater hauling capacity and more effectiveness in negotiating the curvature of the line, ready for departure in 1905.

Behind the North Pier, Stafford Street intersects with the main thoroughfare, George Street. The Oban Inn, built in 1790, lies just out of the cameraman's view on the extreme left; the distillery, one of the many developments of the Stevenson brothers, commenced production four years later. This view of *c*.1903 is crowned by the 630 foot-wide halo of McCaig's Tower (or Folly, as it has often been described).

John Stuart McCaig ('Art Critic and Philosopher, Essayist and Banker'), constructed his tower of Bonawe granite during the closing years of Queen Victoria's reign, funding the reputed cost of £5,000 himself. It was built during the winter months when stonemasons had difficulty in finding employment. There are elements of both altruism and self-aggrandisement in this story, as McCaig apparently intended to place statues of his family in some of the many window niches, but he died in 1902 leaving his lasting legacy to the town incomplete. Over the intervening years the structure has been called 'senseless', 'futile' and 'useless', and some have even called for its removal. However, attitudes change and a gradual reappraisal has emerged so that today McCaig's Tower is considered to be as much a symbol of Oban as the Statue of Liberty is of New York or the Opera House is of Sydney. A superb viewpoint by day, it can be transformed by floodlighting at night into an extraordinarily ethereal spectacle of pure theatre.

George Street, looking north from Stafford Street (above), and (below) the west-facing shops and hotels. Included in the picture are the Kings Arms (1855), the Caledonian (1830) and, at the far left on the corner of Argyll Street, Chalmers Tweed Warehouse (1901). The latter could claim royalty as patrons, and advertised 'tailor-made gowns and coats, sportsman's tailor, tartans, rugs, Scottish woollens and homespuns, and Shetland hand-knit hosiery' – all in all, an attraction which few tourists could resist.

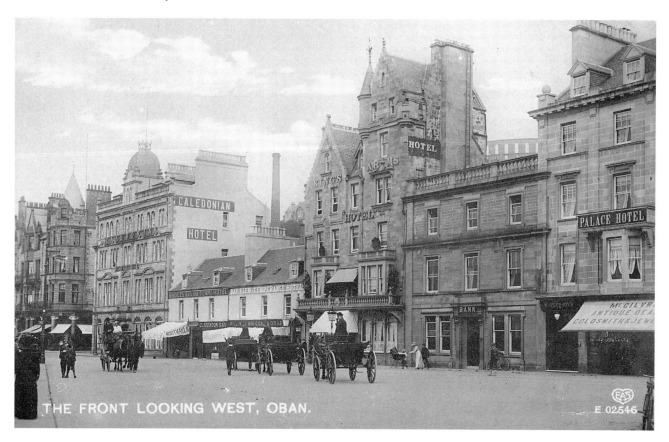

A short distance behind Rockfield Road, and a little above it in height, a plateau tops a rocky eminence known as Oban Hill. At a height of some 200 feet above sea level, the view westwards across Oban Bay to Kerrera and beyond is, as the Glasgow *Evening Times* claimed without exaggeration in October 1881, 'one hardly to be equalled for extent or magnificence'. The prospects are just as superb today, although much has changed on the hilltop itself. The foundations of a large building, with a frontage of about 300 feet, are clearly discernible through the undergrowth of grass, trees, rhododendrons and briar roses which are steadily reclaiming the site for nature. Low walls, door lintels and circular blockwork for a tower protrude and, at one end, a larger section of window openings rise starkly skywards. The bizarre circumstances which resulted in these ruins are worth recounting.

Hydropathy, a method of treating diseases by the use of pure water both internally and externally, was the brainchild of a Silesian peasant, Vincent Priessnitz who in 1829 established an institution for the hydropathic treatment of diseases. He invented a variety of associated water cures including the wet-sheet pack, the dry blanket or sweating pack, the sitz, douche, plunge and wave, all of which were offered alongside a variety of hot- and cold-water baths. The new treatments acquired great popularity and led to 'hydropathics' springing up across Europe, complementing the contemporary enthusiasm for taking cures at spa towns. The establishment of a hydropathic society in London in 1842 resulted in the movement spreading to the United Kingdom. In many instances, patients received lasting benefits at a hydropathic, but by the end of the nineteenth century there was a dawning realisation that the advantages of exercise and diet, which were also part of the regime, were at least as beneficial as the much publicised water treatments.

The coming of the railway in 1880 had brought both Glasgow and Edinburgh within easy reach of Oban, giving a great boost to tourism. The following year, perhaps sensing an opportunity for profit, a group of mainly Glasgow shareholders subscribed to the formation of a new company, the Oban Hills Hydropathic Sanatorium Company, to build a hydropathic hotel in a premier position above the town. The builders, Robert McAlpine & Co., assigned 300 workmen to the project, and materials were to be delivered up to the site by a miniature railway. The design would be in the Scottish Baronial style incorporating 137 bedrooms, a conservatory, concert hall and sea water baths. Externally, plans included provision for stabling, a golf course and a large landscaped garden. A hydraulic lift would bring guests and their luggage up from the town, and sea water would be pumped up from the bay (despite the quality of the water at this time not being a subject considered fit to discuss within these pages!). The building quickly took shape, but somehow the sums increasingly failed to add up. This photograph shows the building at its fullest extent prior to the cessation of work in 1882 when the roof timbers were actually in place. Shareholders were unable or unwilling to invest further monies and the project, despite being so far advanced, was abandoned never to be resumed. The ruins were subsequently pillaged extensively for the villas which were built around the hill. (Photograph reproduced here by kind permission of Robert McCulloch.)

An advertisement for Mackay's well patronised shop in Queen's Park Place, 1910. A magnet for tourists, it stocked everything a visitor might reasonably require, including pocket sized novels priced between 3½d and 1/- in 'Collins beautifully illustrated clear type editions'. A few of the many postcards bearing the Mackay imprint and sold in the shop are shown in this book. Mackay also published his *Complete Tourist Guide to Oban and Vicinity*, incorporating two maps, priced 6d in 1910. My own copy of this edition purchased 90 years later cost exactly 1,000 times the original purchase price; so much for inflation and collectability!

THE ONE-STOREY BLOCK, OBAN.

QUEEN'S PARK PLACE

(Between the Railway Station and N. Pier).

BOOKS.—The Principal **SHOP** where to buy your Books, Bibles, Music Books, Guides, Maps, &c.

STATIONERY.—All Qualities and Sizes, Fancy and Plain.

PICTURE POSTCARDS.—The Largest and best Assortment in Town.

PRESENTS.—Iona and Scotch Pebble Jewellery, Crest China, Writing Cases and Souvenirs of all Kinds.

PHOTOGRAPHS.—Thousands to choose from, also Books of Views, 1/-, 2/6, 12/6 to £5. New Brown Maddotype Photographs, 10d, 2/-, 3/- and 7/6 each.

Sketching Materials.   Golf Balls and Clubs.

Scotch and English Newspapers delivered.

D. **MACKAY**, Bookseller, Stationer and House Agent.

The Royal Hotel, built in 1895, advertised its 'beautiful situation, comfort with moderate charges and excellent cuisine'. Nothing especially original there, perhaps, but the provision of a 'motor garage and inspection pit' were useful facilities, no doubt, for the increasing numbers of motoring guests staying there before the Great War.

Oban   The Royal Hotel

The Columba Hotel, conspicuously sited on North Pier, began life as Columba Terrace in 1864.

These photographs show the two architecturally very different parts of the hotel, the later section incorporating the conveniently placed MacBrayne's Steam Packet Office, and several shops including Chalmers Royal Tartan House. Above the dairy, on the southern elevation, a stone tablet records the date of building, AD 1902.

These interior scenes – the drawing room, billiard room and lounge – appeared in Mackay's *Tourist Guide* of 1910 when the hotel had been 'fitted up with all the latest improvements' and was under the new management of A. Hemm (Proprietor).

Impressive, imposing and grand are words which might readily spring to mind in describing the Great Western Hotel on Corran Esplanade. Advertisements prior to 1914 claimed it to be 'the largest and leading hotel in the Western Highlands', having an 'unrivalled position facing the bay and yacht anchorage'. Built to the designs of Charles Wilson of Glasgow in 1862, it has not only been cited as the finest example of surviving Victorian hotel architecture in the town, but also as the first hotel in Oban to have been lit by electricity.

These photographs of the entrance hall (centre) and drawing room (right) portray a fondness for potted palms and all the lavishness and opulence so typical of the closing years of the nineteenth century.

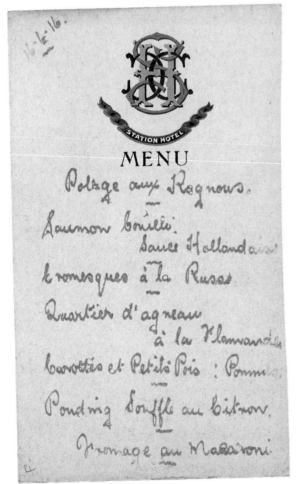

Built about 1880, the Station Hotel underwent a change of name in the early 1960s becoming the Caledonian Hotel. This unusual postcard, bearing a line drawing of the hotel, was produced by Chr. Weiersmüller of Nürnberg and displays on the reverse . . .

. . . a menu from the dining room dated 16 June 1916 – ample proof that two years after the outbreak of the Great War, there was no shortage of good fare for diners here!

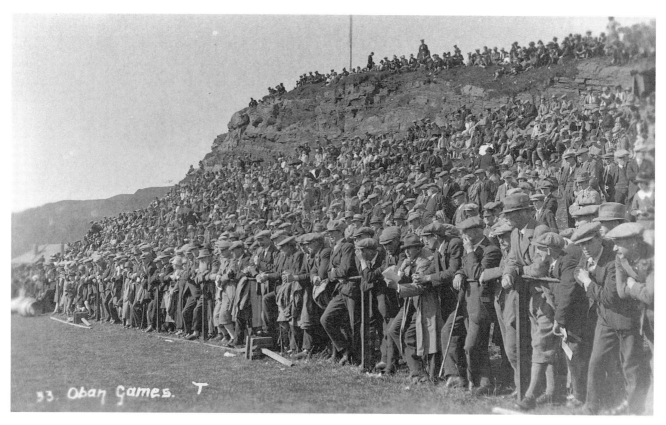

33 Oban Games.

Henry Scrivens' crowd scene at the Oban Games around the hill at Soroba provides a valuable social record of the dress code in the 1920s, inviting comparison with our own less formal times. Most gentlemen wear a tie, and only a very few heads are uncovered. Between and behind the fifth and sixth persons on the rail (from the right) even a soldier's medals are visible. Part of the ethos surrounding the events comprising the Argyllshire Gathering was about being seen.

The Scrivens' studio at the northern end of George Street. He recorded many local social events, people at work and at play, including scenes at the annual Oban Games where he would photograph not only competitors, but also sections of the crowd. Later people would flock to The Studio to examine his photographs, displayed in the windows and on the counter, attempting to identify themselves. (Photograph reproduced here by kind permission of Robert McCulloch.)

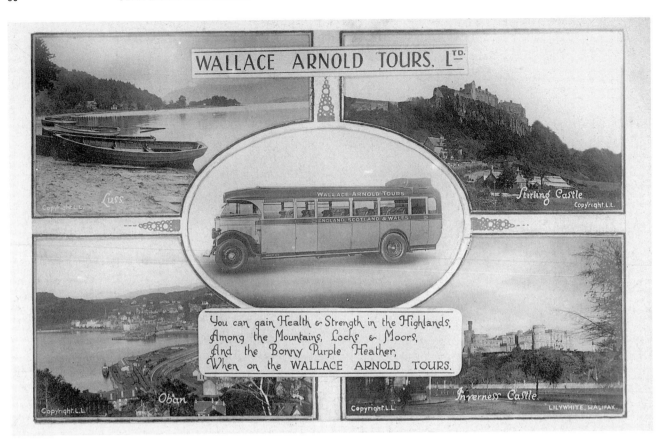

In 1922, Wallace Arnold of Leeds advertised five-day coach tours to Edinburgh for £8.8/- and a nine-day tour of the Scottish Highlands for exactly twice that sum. Their last open charabanc was withdrawn in 1928 when the tour fleet became 'all weather', the coaches having enclosed bodywork and pneumatic tyres which provided a smoother ride at the 20 mph maximum speed then permitted. Couriers and travelling rugs made their appearance; stops were made at exclusive hotels.

In 1870 livestock auctions commenced in Oban, but sending cattle to the market there was always a lottery for the islesmen. Shipped in, their animals were often distressed by the journey, and poor condition on arrival would ultimately be reflected in the prices offered to the seller, who had little alternative but to accept what was offered. Return transport involving further cost was not an option. 'We saw a cattle boat unloading this morning; the poor animals were soaked with sea water and all crowded on deck. The men had such a trouble to drive them off', wrote one bystander before the Great War. This flock of sheep, just unloaded, is probably destined for market.

254. Landing The Herring At Oban.

The fishing industry has always been of vital importance to – if not the very foundation of – so many west coast communities. In the 1880s, the new pier facilities at the Oban railhead built by the Callander and Oban Railway began to attract the Stornoway fish traffic away from the company's rivals, the Highland Railway, and their landing ports further north. These Scrivens' photographs show aspects associated with the herring catch.

Hours spent gutting and grading deep farlins of herring ('the silver darlings') was back-breaking work for the fisher lassies, sometimes described as the unsung heroines of the fishing industry. Girls began gutting between the ages of 15 and 18 years, and while some followed the boats on the annual migration of the herring

Fisher Girls, Oban.

shoals around the British Isles, others stayed at just one location for the season. Skilled girls could gut up to 60 herrings a minute, but despite the hard work, long hours and poor pay, camaraderie was good.

249. Packing The Fish For Despatch

Packing and boxing-up. A perfect combination; the fish are packed in Hailstones and ice! Apart from herring, other fish including white fish were landed here. During the first half of the twentieth century, Alexander Leslie (known throughout Lorn as the 'Lobster King') had a thriving business based in Horse Shoe Bay on Kerrera, and at Cullipool on the island of Luing, where in a tidal pond Leslie might store up to 50,000 lobsters at a time. Whether fish or lobster, much of the catch went south by overnight train bound for London and the southern markets, destined for diners' plates at top restaurants or even aboard the prestigious Cunard liners. The *Queen Mary* and *Queen Elizabeth* would commence their fortnightly round trips with some 2,000 lbs of Kerrera lobsters aboard.

Titled 'The New Promenade Extension', this photograph shows 'The Plateau' (a name once applied to this area) at the far end of Dunollie Esplanade, with the castle in the background. A man eyes the cameraman suspiciously as his companion gazes out to sea, while behind them, another takes a siesta, *c.*1903.

This picture was taken at the same spot as the one above (but looking in the opposite direction), and it was here the Duke of Argyll officially opened the new road to Ganavan in 1903. The construction of this road necessitated the relocation of the weighty boulder shown here lying on its side. Tradition associates Fingal, a great warrior-hero of Gaelic romance with the huge Dogstone nearby, and appropriately perhaps, this much smaller one with his son Ossian.

After the Great War, Ossian's Putting Stone was placed upright and incorporated into the fine memorial designed by Alexander Carrick RSA to honour the 174 men who did not return. Of these, very nearly one-third had served with the Argyll and Sutherland Highlanders.

The Brooch
of
Lorne

M'Isaac & Riddle, Oban.

"Whence the brooch of burning gold,
That clasps the Chieftain's mantle fold,
Wrought and chased with rare device,
Studded fair with gems of price?"

The Lord of The Isles.
Scott.

The Brooch of Lorne has been described as the finest specimen of Scoto-Scandinavian art preserved in Britain; a priceless relic, without doubt, it now belongs to MacDougall of MacDougall. Snatched by a dying clansman from the plaid of the King of Scotland, Robert the Bruce, at the desperate skirmish at Dalrigh (Strathfillan) in August 1306, the brooch was claimed as a trophy of war by John of Lorn and remained a MacDougall possession until being carried off during the sacking of Gylen Castle on Kerrera in 1647. For the next 179 years, until 1826, the brooch appears to have been in Campbell hands when, owing to the good offices of General Duncan Campbell of Lochnell, it was generously returned without reservation to the MacDougall family. This early twentieth century photograph by McIsaac and Riddle of Oban is complemented by the late Seton Gordon's description of the brooch: 'The large crystal set in that old brooch is unusual. Under whatever conditions of light it may be viewed, a warm glow, as from a peat fire, burns within its depths. Surrounding the large central crystal are a number of pearls, set in a circle. The centre of the brooch unscrews, and within is a small box which formerly contained a small piece of bone (perhaps a saintly relic) and a piece of very old MacDougall tartan, hand-spun and much faded.'

The ruins of Dunollie Castle, crowned by the familiar square shape of the surviving fifteenth century keep, perch on a rocky promontory 80 feet above Port Mór. Virtually impregnable, the castle was unsuccessfully besieged in 1647. The site is, however, believed to be a much older one having been occupied by primitive fortifications as early as the seventh century. The present ruins incorporate walls with an average thickness of 10 feet, and of the original enceinte only those of the north and east remain.

Two years after the battle at Dalrigh, The Bruce took his revenge by routing a large force of MacDougalls, incurring great loss of life, in the Pass of Brander. This decisive defeat signalled a swift decline in the fortunes of the clan and a loss of influence in their Lorn heartland. Most of their island possessions were sequestered and reassigned to MacDonald, Lord of the Isles, while in 1388 the Lordship of Lorn which included Lismore, Appin, Benderloch and Dunstaffnage passed by marriage to the Stewarts. The waning influence of the MacDougalls created a vacuum which would soon be filled by Clan Campbell; their dominance over the region became total.

DUNOLLIE CASTLE, SHEPHERDS HAT AND MOUNTAINS OF MULL, OBAN. 2|549|.

This photograph illustrates perfectly the strategic and commanding setting of Dunollie Castle, overlooking the sea lanes around Kerrera (left), Lismore, and across the Firth of Lorn to Mull. Despite the chequered fortunes of the Clan, these historic lands remain the seat of MacDougall of MacDougall, Chief of the Clan, who lives in a house built *c.*1746 in the shadow of the ruined castle.

Ganavan Sands, Oban

87587. COPYRIGHT.

Much development has taken place here since this photograph was taken, but in the early days of motoring it must have been a joy to take a drive out to Ganavan Sands from Oban. An invigorating walk by the shore, or a ramble along the cliffs, might sharpen up the appetite for afternoon tea – and what better way to round off the day back in town than by visiting Kennedy's well-known lunch and tea rooms at 60 George Street?

Tradition associates Dunstaffnage as a northern seat of the ancient Dalriadan kingdom, and with the Stone of Destiny, although the royal residence was abandoned in the ninth century. Guarding the approaches to Loch Etive, the present castle (illustrated here) was built by the MacDougalls in the thirteenth century; massive curtain walls enclose towers and a gatehouse of later date which can be viewed from a parapet walk above the inner courtyard. Following the seizure of MacDougall lands, the Campbells became Captains of the castle. Flora MacDonald, the Skye heroine who assisted the escape of Bonnie Prince Charlie, was imprisoned here for ten days in 1746 en route to London. I understand that Michael Campbell, the 22nd Hereditary Captain of Dunstaffnage, is required to spend at least one night a year in the castle to retain his title! In woods close by, a chapel (c.1225) consisting of ruined nave, chancel and burial aisle exudes an atmosphere of great antiquity.

Connel Ferry from the south c.1890. This was a ferrying point from distant times, and either side of the narrows two inns serving as ferry-houses once provided refreshment for travellers. The ancient slipways became redundant on the building of the Connel Ferry Bridge, in the shadow of which they now lie. The Moss of Achnacree and the lands of Benderloch lie across the mouth of Loch Etive.

Based at the Railway Pier, Oban, and owned by Alexander Paterson (and later by his son until 1935), SS *Princess Louise* undertook service runs to Dunstaffnage and Connel Ferry, where she is seen here. Her work also included excursions to Kerrera, and the shipping of livestock from the islands of Coll and Colonsay.

At Connel a reef of rocks stretches out across the Loch Etive narrows where the tidal waters ebb and flow. The celebrated Falls of Lora, of Ossian song and story – in reality more properly described as rapids or cataracts – occur at this rock barrier which at ebb tide is covered to a depth of only six feet. Above the rapids, the depth reaches 420 feet in the huge rock basin of the loch, while on the seaward side it gradually increases to 168 feet at a distance of 2 miles. An ebb tide flowing across the reef at some 10 to 12 knots is capable of producing a roar which can be heard over a considerable distance. I cannot confirm a claim that these are the only *saltwater* falls in the world, but offer it as a comment for discussion.

Built by the Arrol Bridge Company between 1898 and 1903, the single cantilever span of the Connel Ferry Bridge was the supreme engineering achievement of the stunningly scenic 28 mile branch railway line to Ballachulish. Incorporating some 2,600 tons of steel, no rail bridge in Great Britain had a longer main span at the time of its construction except that of the Forth Bridge. The railway was carried high above the Falls of Lora where the width of the waterway at this narrow neck of Loch Etive measured 690 feet, the span being supported by three arched masonry viaducts either side of the loch. This photograph, showing the central section still incomplete, has the added interest of being signed on the reverse by H. Cecil-Booth (Engineer in Charge of Construction), and is dated 1903. (Photograph reproduced here by kind permission of Robin Buchanan-Smith.)

In June 1914 a roadway to accommodate motor cars was opened alongside the track (with access restricted to prevent road and rail traffic from using the bridge simultaneously); this private photograph taken through a car windscreen during a crossing on the bridge illustrates these arrangements. Toll charges ranged from 7/6d to 10/-. Following the closure of the railway in 1966, the Connel Ferry Bridge was converted solely to road use, the one-way traffic being controlled by lights at either end.

Overlooking its own gardens and Loch Etive, the Falls of Lora Hotel (seen here *c*.1900) was built in a typically solid, architecturally-pleasing Victorian style, and elegantly furnished within. It was later enlarged. A picture of Murdoch MacGillvray, who purchased the site and built the hotel in 1886 to meet the increasing demands of visitors, hangs by the reception desk. Quite understandably, he was apparently not best pleased as the building of the new bridge took shape within sight of his windows, obscuring the formerly uninterrupted views of North Connel.

Connel Ferry Station lies just behind the hotel. Passengers reaching Connel from the south would have a sense of anticipation for it was not only the junction for the Ballachulish line, but also the last stopping place before Oban. A double-headed train lies by the platform on 19 August 1939, the photograph being marked quite simply 'Our train to Oban'. Maybe the start of a happy holiday – if so, perhaps the last for some time, as within days and for the second time in a century, the world was about to be plunged into years of war.

Achnacloich (the 'field of stones') lies 3 miles east of Connel on the southern shore of Loch Etive. In the upper of these two late Victorian photographs, the peak of Ben Cruachan pierces the skyline, while in the foreground a road leads down from the station building to the pier where the SS *Ossian* is moored. During the summer months the morning and afternoon steamer trips to Loch Etive Head proved popular combined rail and sea excursions from Oban. Views of Ardchattan Priory, Airds Point, the quarries at Bonawe and the scattered, remote, roadless settlements by the lochside, coupled with an opportunity to stretch one's legs at the pierhead near the mountains of Glencoe – and the possibility of seeing that most majestic of birds, the golden eagle – all made for a memorable outing. Fares for 1910 were: first class train and steamer (cabin) 5/6*d*.; third Class 4/6*d*.

An invoice relating to the repair of SS *Ossian*'s ship's clock in 1910.

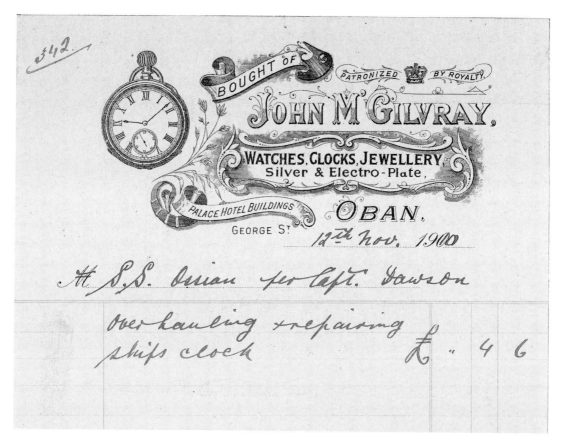

Lying just outside the village on the main road, the Taynuilt Hotel was once a change-house and a stage for the Inverary to Oban mails. The importance of this posting establishment can be gauged from the range of outbuildings, which included large stone stables incorporating overnight quarters for coachmen, and an old laundry. The Glen Nant coach and the coaches which met the Loch Etive steamers and took their passengers on to Loch Awe and Glencoe were also stabled here.

At Tailor's Leap in wooded Glen Nant on the Taynuilt to Kilchrenan road, tradition relates how a distiller of illicit whisky leapt across 40-foot falls in the river to avoid capture by excisemen, apparently not a totally unique feat in the Highlands! The photographs taken at this favourite stopping-place show the Glen Nant coach c.1900, and a group of motor charabanc tourists posing on the road in the 1920s for another Henry Scrivens picture.

Whether on the mainland or the islands, those raising cattle faced a common problem when it came to trading and selling. Stock had to be taken to a distant market, and long before the days of mechanised transport that meant, quite simply, driving cattle overland and ferrying them across water. To witness a drove of a couple of hundred, or perhaps a thousand head on the move, must indeed have been a spectacle. The drovers used the historic 'green roads' of glen and strath – remote ways and passes known only to pilgrim and packman since earliest times – and their pace was a leisurely 10 to 12 miles per day as beasts needed to be rested and watered in order to reach market in good condition, otherwise prices would suffer. Several historic droving routes bisected Lorn, passing both around and across Loch Awe. The Glen Nant and Midmuir drove roads came through Kilchrenan (top) where Tigh Ban, now a private residence, was once an inn and change-house. At nearby Taychreggan, cattle were swum or ferried across the loch and rested at Portsonachan on the eastern shore, before continuing their overland journey to the Falkirk Tryst.

At Taychreggan, the road ends at a small jetty alongside a comfortable hotel, a building which is believed to have replaced an earlier inn known to the cattle drovers of old. At times between May and October large numbers of beasts would have congregated along the shoreline here to await a crossing of Loch Awe, a continuous operation often lasting several days at a time. Both photographs date to the first few years of the last century.

Portsonachan (the 'Blessed Port') lies eastwards across Loch Awe and is glimpsed here from Taychreggan jetty *c*.1904. The drove went this way, and for centuries a small passenger ferry plied these waters, ceasing only towards the end of the Second World War.

Portsonachan Hotel and jetty *c*.1900. Malcolm of Poltalloch purchased the estate in the nineteenth century and built the hotel on the site of an older inn. These days both the Taychreggan and Portsonachan hotels are well geared to the particular requirements of fishermen. Weighty catches are evidenced by the display of some superb wall-mounted specimens at the former.

SS *Caledonia* at Portsonachan *c.*1910. This little passenger steamer, together with others, linked several points on the northern part of Loch Awe with the Glen Nant coach at Taychreggan and the railway station in Lochawe village. Using a combination of horse-drawn coach, steamer and railway it was then possible to undertake a round-trip from Oban via Taynuilt in either direction, making in the words of one guide 'a little gem of a tour which may be accomplished in six hours'.

'On Loch Awe Side' depicts a couple of hovels by the lochside; the message on the reverse is quite priceless. Posted at Taynuilt on 26 August 1909 and addressed to Miss M. McFarlane, The Hydropathic (note spelling), Moffat, the message reads: 'I have just heard from Barney – she is in <u>Leipzig</u> again. However do you think she managed it! I have written and asked her to explain how she manages these things and I shall try them on too! Truly fortune favours not the <u>brave</u> but the specially ugly. Today is very wet and stormy and I wish I were home – any place but this hole. Love from Margaret.'

Ford lies at the southernmost point of Loch Awe's 24-mile length, on the line of a historic drove road and major trading route through mid-Argyll from Craignish and Kintraw in the west, and via Kilneuair over Leacan Muir eastwards to Inverary and beyond. Opposite the Ford Hotel (1864), formerly named the Auchinellan Inn, there was once a large cattle stance. *Top:* In 1876 SS *Lochawe* (seen here at Ford Pier) was brought to Ford in sections for reassembly. Her regular calls included New York (on the west bank of Loch Awe), Portsonachan, Cladich and Lochawe Pier on the opening of the railway in 1880. Her last run was in August 1914; thereafter she lay at Ford Pier until she was scrapped 10 years later. *Above:* Faces peer from an upstairs window and a man seated on a bench by the doorway watches the photographer as he composes this scene outside the Ford Hotel *c.*1908.

Ederline.

The Ederline Estate, Ford: the 'big house' and Clachandhu Cottages. While the eighteenth century mansion remains at Ederline, the impressive, noble Scottish Baronial pile of 1870 (the seat of the Warde-Aldams family) whose windows overlooked Loch Ederline, was demolished in 1966. There is a certain irony here, as the former agricultural workers' cottages in the shadow of Clachandhu Hill (below, photographed by a Yorkshire photographer in the early years of the last century), are still extant.

OBAN to DUNADD

In the vast, complex jigsaw of land and water between Oban and Dunadd there are no towns; small, scattered and sometimes remote settlements predominate, interspersed by a number of estates and their 'big houses'. The black cattle for which Argyll was famous were raised on the islands and in the hills, glens and straths of this western seaboard. The historic drove roads of Mull, Kerrera, Islay and Jura joined those which criss-crossed mainland Argyll enabling beasts to be driven to market. The rugged coast and heavily indented hinterland is pierced by the ancient drowned valleys of Lochs Feochan, Melfort and Craignish, while strewn across the ocean are the numerous islands, reefs and skerries of Nether Lorn, some having early religious associations, others remaining monuments to an industrial past. Indeed, the third former great manufacturing industry of Lorn to be featured in this book, namely the extraction of slate, was centred on the islands of Seil, Easdale, Luing and Belnahua (collectively known as the Slate Islands) whose resources have been commercially exploited since the seventeenth century. Further out to sea lie the Garvellachs (Isles of the Sea or Holy Islands) associated with the early saints, Brendan and Columba. St Adamnan, an early Abbot of Iona, was Columba's seventh-century biographer. Is the island of Eileach an Naoimh, with its ruined monastery and beehive cells (clochains), the sacred Hinba (Insula Hinbinae) of his *Life of Columba* – the rocky retreat to which the saint was wont to repair for solitude, meditation and prayer? Such claims have found broad agreement among the greatest authorities on the subject. Elsewhere, those who sail the waters around these dangerous coasts with their ever-changing panorama of islands, need to be well acquainted with some exceptional features marked on their navigational charts – the Dorus Mor (the 'Great Sea Gate') between Craignish Point and the island of Garbh Reisa, and the fearsome whirlpool of Corrievreckan (between Jura and Scarba) whose roar, likened to distant thunder, may in certain conditions be heard up to 20 miles away. The many surviving prehistoric monuments to be found in the landscape around Kilmartin testify to human occupation since earliest times, while nearby Dunadd was a supremely significant site 1,500 years ago when it was the centre of the ancient kingdom of Dalriada, and the first capital of Scotland.

The puffer *Sunflower* at South Pier, Oban *c.*1900. Such small, shallow-draught vessels were ideal for conveying and delivering bulky cargoes, often coal, to the more isolated mainland and island locations along the coastline of Argyll. A gently shelving sandy beach made an ideal landing-place; the cargo would be offloaded at low tide directly into horse-drawn carts, prior to distribution around the district.

Oban from West.

The two ladies walking in Gallanach Road *c*.1910 are nearing the Lighthouse Pier and, out of sight, the Manor House, built in 1780 as a principal residence of the Duke of Argyll's Oban Estate. The small white building they have just passed, the Piermaster's House (built 1814, and also shown in the previous picture) is the town's earliest surviving harbour building. The area around South Pier is much changed today.

The area adjacent to the Manor House became a major depot for the Northern Lighthouse Board for all manner of stores, as well as providing a berth for the *Hesperus* from 1907. This ship was one of several operated by the Board to service the many lighthouses, minor lights and buoys around the Scottish coasts, as well as undertaking the transfer of

lighthousemen to provide periodic relief for their colleagues manning often remote stations. Spells ashore were always welcomed. Each landing presented its own particular problems and challenges to the captain and crew of such ships, who had intimate knowledge of the stations they relieved. Changing times have resulted in the automation of all lights in these waters, and these days maintenance staff are often landed by helicopter.

At Kilbowie Gates, Gallanach Road. The coach house and stables, together with some staff accommodation (left), lay immediately opposite the entrance to the 'big house'. Very considerable changes have taken place since this picture was taken a hundred years ago, and the ivy-covered stone gate pillars have vanished, along with much else.

Detailed as Kilbowie Lodge in the valuation rolls, this rather fine mansion in the Scottish Baronial style, incorporating ornate conservatories, was built in 1880 by Alexander Dunn Pattison of Dalmuir. The neat grounds, contained within the long stone wall by the roadside, ran parallel to the shore overlooking Kerrera. The property continued to be the Dunn Pattisons' family home until the closing years of Queen Victoria's reign. A century later, residential development has taken place in the grounds, part of which are used as the Kilbowie Outdoor Centre, while the Lodge now houses the offices of the Argyll and Bute Roads Department.

Kerrera was once a stepping-stone for the shipment of cattle between Auchnacraig (Mull) and the mainland, the final stage of the sea journey being the ¾-mile tideway between Port Kerrera and Ardbhan (pictured c.1900). The drove continued over the hills (extreme right) via Lochan na Croise, Cleigh and Kilmore to join the Midmuir Drove Road for Taychreggan. Long before the development of Oban, Kerrera folk also took this ferry to attend church at Kilmore (see page 84), trekking the 4 miles through these same hills, the round trip involving a whole day.

Kerrera is 4½ miles in length, varies in width from 300 yards to nearly 2 miles, and supported a peak population of 187 in 1841. The old ferry-house at Port Kerrera, set in an elevated position above Horse Shoe Bay, was already a provider of local services when, in 1879, additional responsibilities were assumed. The General Post Office in Edinburgh authorised the establishment of a sub-post office on the island to handle the local mail, which arrived via Oban and was brought over three times a week on the ferry-boat. This photograph (c.1930) shows the ferry-house/post office on the left, the school (right, built in 1872) which also doubled as the church, and the teacher's house (centre). The post office closed in November 1969.

Dramatically sited on a sheer-sided promontory on the south of the island, Gylen Castle, although ruined, is still a major landmark. Described as 'a little architectural gem', it was built as a fortified residence and MacDougall stronghold using the varied rock available locally, and is thought to date from 1582. Gylen had a short history, as only 65 years later the castle was successfully besieged by General Leslie who, as related earlier, carried off everything of value including the Brooch of Lorne which had been lodged there for safe keeping.

Kilmore Post Office lay by the River Nell at Cleigh, on the main coast road 3½ miles south of Oban. Once an important mail collection and delivery point for the scattered population around Loch Nell and Glen Feochan, it has long since closed and reverted to a private residence. The sender of this postcard *c.*1910 considered it 'a splendid place for courting'. Well!

Mr Mackay of Oban photographed the old mill on the River Nell (centre) and the Feochan Inn (right) about 1904. Situated at Cleigh, the inn was once the site of a noted change-house where drovers rested and watered their beasts on the long overland journey to their final destination at the huge cattle trysts at Crieff and Falkirk.

'People here cross ferries and ride great distances in bad weather not only to hear sermons but also to converse together and hear all the news of friends at home and abroad' – so wrote Mrs Grant of Laggan in her *Letters from the Mountains*, following her attendance at a service in the Old Church of Kilmore in 1773. The church in Glen Feochan is first recorded in 1304, although the existing building, which had no division between nave and chancel, dates from the fifteenth or sixteenth century. The parishes of Kilmore and nearby Kilbride were united in 1638, but the last services were held in 1876. The former places of worship still survive in both parishes, but only as ruins.

Glenfeochan House *c*.1900. The house, surrounded by 350 acres of hills, woods and pasture is set back some distance from the road skirting Loch Feochan. Built in 1875, the property displays interesting features externally, while inside, the well-proportioned rooms have ceilings of extravagantly ornate plasterwork in the manner of the period. Some years ago, I recall that the then owners made Herculean efforts to restore to their former glory the 1½ acre walled garden, the sadly neglected and overgrown policies with their specimen trees, and the Victorian arboretum.

The Melfort to Oban coach makes an unscheduled stop by Loch Feochan about a century ago, while an unknown photographer, closely watched by the driver, sets up his camera in the road. The return excursion to the Pass of Melfort was, declared Mackay's Guide, 'of all the coaching tours from Oban, indisputably the finest'. Leaving MacGregor's Coach Office at Station Hotel Buildings at 10.30 a.m., Kilninver was reached at 11.40 and the Cuilfail Hotel at 1.10 p.m., where refreshments were available. Returning from the hotel at 3.20 p.m., Oban was reached by 6 p.m. Fare 7/-, with an extra 1/- for guard and driver.

Passengers on the motor-bus admire views across Loch Feochan to the mountains of Mull. The vehicle signboard – Oban, Melfort, Ford and Lochawe – advertises another popular excursion which offered the prospect of a sail up the length of the loch, coupled with 'an excellent lunch in the airy cabin of the SS "Lochawe" '. This trip could be taken on either a 'there and back' basis or made a circular by returning to Oban by train from Lochawe Station. Endless enticing excursions were available throughout the area by using permutations of coach or motor transport combined with steamer and rail travel.

Buildings can be fascinating: some remain entirely as built, some are enlarged or reduced in size, while others may be demolished. This house at Knipoch, however, is *hidden*. I stood outside the Knipoch Hotel with the receptionist amid the growing realisation that the old house had been skilfully incorporated into the hotel's northern end during the enlargement undertaken in the 1930s and 1980s, where it remains disguised under a harmonised roof level and a colour co-ordinated frontage. A metal plaque bearing the date 1635, possibly a fireback, was found during the renovations and has now been wall-mounted in the Stone Room, approximately behind the figures in this 1920s photograph.

At one time the main Oban to Melfort road entered Kilninver, passing the church and a local signpost marked 'Melfort'. The subsequent realignment of roads resulted in the village being bypassed and the erection of a new sign which today indicates Campbeltown, more than 80 miles distant. Someone takes great interest examining the side of the bridge in this Henry Scrivens photograph, taken about 70 years ago. A few yards behind the photographer . . .

. . . lies Kilninver Post Office on the road to Seil and Easdale; as at Kilmore, it has now closed. The loss of such facilities results in the diminution of the quality of life for so many in rural areas, and strikes a resonant chord with our own times when such closures remain an issue.

Ardmaddy Castle *c.*1905. A late medieval tower-house dating from the fifteenth century may have been the original building on this rocky eminence at the head of Ardmaddy Bay, an inlet of the Sound of Seil. Subsequently enlarged in the eighteenth and nineteenth centuries, influential architects included James Gillespie Graham and David Bryce. About 1648 ownership passed from the MacDougalls to the Campbells, and later to the Breadalbane family for whom Ardmaddy became a principal residence until the disposal of the estate in 1933. During the late 1970s the central portion of the castle was demolished, leaving the tower detached. Should you see the date AD 1929 on the surviving portion, partially obscured by a tree (right), do not be deceived, as this merely relates to a window opening. Argyll is justly famous for its gardens: those at Ardmaddy are generally open to the public.

In 1791 John Stevenson of Oban was building this graceful, high-arched stone bridge linking the Island of Seil with the mainland (foreground) at Clachan. The 70-foot span rises to a height of 40 feet above the seabed of that part of the Atlantic Ocean – otherwise known as Clachan Sound – a fact which, in the early days, gave credence to the claim that it was 'the only bridge over the Atlantic'. The building costs of approximately £450 were shared between Lord Breadalbane, MacDougall of Ardencaple and the Easdale Slate Company. The Tigh-an-Truish Inn, the 'House of the Trews' (left) is said to have gained its name following the 'Forty-five' when the wearing of the kilt was proscribed; non-compliance was an offence punishable by execution. Local islesmen bound for the mainland would leave 'incriminating' clothing here, donning plain trousers as demanded by law, and collecting their kilts on the return journey.

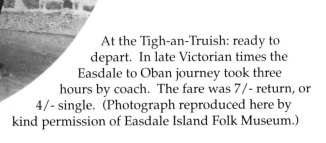

At the Tigh-an-Truish: ready to depart. In late Victorian times the Easdale to Oban journey took three hours by coach. The fare was 7/- return, or 4/- single. (Photograph reproduced here by kind permission of Easdale Island Folk Museum.)

Balvicar crossroads and Clachandubh
Farmhouse *c*.1898. The sight of a row of
cottages once lived in by the quarriers at
Balvicar is likely to be the visitor's first
acquaintance with what was formerly a
great industry of Lorn, the production of
roofing slates. For the geologist, the
islands collectively known as 'The Slate
Islands' are of considerable interest.
Millions of years ago gigantic forces caused
upheavals in the earth's crust leaving
formations of slate near or below ground
level in this part of Argyll. Those wishing
to know more of such matters, and the life
and work of the locality, will be well-
rewarded by visiting both the Ellenabeich
Heritage Centre and Easdale Island Folk
Museum, the latter a mere 3 minutes
sailing time by ferry. (Photograph
reproduced here by kind permission of
Easdale Island Folk Museum.)

The terraced cottages of Ellenabeich's old distillery (foreground) seen here in 1905, made way about 1930 for
An Cala, a house built for Lt. Col. the Hon. Arthur Murray (later Lord Elibank), set in sheltered gardens
landscaped by Thomas Mawson. Beds of slate either side of the channel separating the mainland from Easdale
Island (top left) have been commercially worked since the seventeenth century. The population of both
communities totalled 756 in 1881. Note the rows of quarriers' cottages, and the former quarry manager's
house (extreme right), now the Inshaig Hotel. Such industrial activity once made Easdale of greater economic
importance than the 'straggling fishing village of Oban'.

7569.   Bird's Eye View of Easdale Island and Ellenabeich.

Water-filled workings at Ellenabeich *c.*1930. Slate was worked vertically, the quarry floor becoming progressively deeper, eventually reaching a depth of 300 feet below sea-level. Terrifyingly, during the night of 21–22 November 1881, a hurricane-force storm accompanied by an abnormal flood tide breached a narrow rock wall, engulfing the workings and machinery and flooding cottages. Commercial quarrying was subsequently intensified on Easdale Island and continued for another 30 years. Production was estimated to have peaked at 9 million slates in 1869. The old steamer pier (centre) is now disintegrating; the crane, just visible, is currently being preserved for posterity. Slate no longer pays the wages here.

Centre: Easdale slate is impregnated with iron pyrites (fool's gold), and when split is somewhat thicker than that quarried elsewhere. Slates were graded by size and stacked on the island's quay (built *c.*1826) awaiting shipment – by the *Dunlop* in this photograph of 1905.

Left: Built in 1866, the twin-funnelled paddle steamer *Chevalier* was for many years closely identified with the Corpach to Crinan service, becoming a familiar sight in Easdale waters. Contemporary reports highlight her 'beautiful lines, flaming red funnels and polished copper steam pipes gleaming in the sun'. She came to grief in Loch Fyne and was scrapped in 1927.

In 1881 agriculture, fishing and quarrying supported a population of over 500 on the neighbouring island of Luing, reached by ferry over Cuan Sound. This photograph of 1904, taken at Toberonochy, illustrates the winning of slate from a deep quarry into which men, lowered on platforms, drilled and blasted the rock face (right), producing material for splitting and knapping. An excellent model portraying such operations and made by Jean Adams, curator of the museum, is on display at Ellenabeich Heritage Centre.

As at Ellenabeich, the pier at Blackmill Bay, on the west coast of Luing, once saw many comings and goings, being an important staging post for shipping including the PS *Chevalier*. Now extensively dilapidated, it presents a sorry spectacle.

The settlement at Cullipool, as it was a century ago, when slate extraction was so important. Puffers transported roofing slates to Glasgow, returning with bulky cargoes, including coal. The famous tidal lobster ponds referred to on page 62 are still in use today. On Belnahua, an island 1½ miles offshore, the ruins of an industrial past are also all too evident. Heritage trail leaflets covering much of the Slate Islands are obtainable at Ellenabeich.

Back on the mainland beyond Kilninver, the River Oude, accompanied by the old road, entered a steep-sided wooded defile at the Pass of Melfort (pictured here *c*.1900) – always a popular halt for a photograph. The gradual 1½ mile descent from the top of the Pass to Loch Melfort was spectacular, the road clinging to the left side of the ravine midway between the river-bed and the ridge. This excursion from Oban was a 'must' for Victorian and Edwardian tourists, and there would be much to talk about over lunch when the Cuilfail Hotel was reached at 1.10 p.m.

A rock-fall in the Pass of Melfort has blocked the road, breaching the retaining wall above the River Oude. Such occurrences were not altogether unusual, especially after periods of heavy rain, and were a factor in the subsequent re-routing of the main coast road *c*.1930. Fortunately for us, Henry Scrivens was on hand with his camera to record this most graphic of scenes.

An early advertising postcard featuring the well-known Cuilfail Hotel. About 1930, a visitor was admiring the spring bulbs and monkey-puzzles in the gardens opposite, 'when the snow came in big, wet flakes, and in two minutes the land was white. In the hotel lounge we found a hospitable fireside and tea, not forgetting a welcome from the host. We stayed much too long. The snow had cleared away, but the light was failing when we took the new road overlooking the Pass of Melfort, where the steep hillside sometimes lets go a few tons of rock on the old' (*Scotland's Rainbow West*, by J. J. Bell).

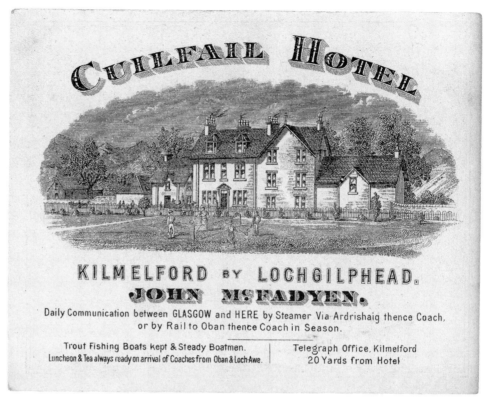

Ghillies (the 'steady boatmen', perhaps?) at the Cuilfail Hotel, *c*.1905. Contemporary reports speak of 'extraordinary takes of splendid trout' from the Oude and smaller streams, as well as from the many lochs and lochans around Melfort.

Melfort House, overlooking Fearnach Bay, an inlet of Loch Melfort, c.1890. By the roadside, around the head of the loch, a post erected by the Road Trust indicates the high water mark reached on 22 November 1881; that same tidal surge which inundated the quarries at Ellenabeich caused serious flooding here. Melfort is notable in other respects, however. Two beautifully-worked Bronze Age (c.1500 BC) metal armlets with a magnificent crescent-shaped necklace of jet were uncovered near the house – priceless treasures now deposited in museums. In 1838 a gunpowder works was established in the valley of the Oude, east and north-east of the 'big house', water power being used to grind and mix the imported ingredients of sulphur and saltpetre with locally produced charcoal. A gigantic explosion destroyed the complex in 1867, although traces of ruined buildings and remnants of a tramway to the pier are still discernible.

Further south at Lunga House, I met Colin Lindsay-MacDougall who told me that the property was originally built as a late fifteenth century dower house belonging to Craignish Castle, 4 miles distant. The MacDougalls moved here from Lunga Island about 1690, and the house became a main seat 30 years later. The estate currently comprises some 4,000 acres, and the ten formerly individual farms are now worked as one.

Loch Craignish. Using the man in the centre of the group as a yardstick, one can estimate the combined height of this solitary standing stone, above and below ground, at 20 feet perhaps! Dating from around 2000 BC, such stones also occur in groups or circles; some mark graves, battlefields or boundaries, while others may have acted as an aid for solar or stellar calculations enabling the passage of the seasons to be measured.

Time to stand and stare – and being able to take a photograph having first parked one's vehicle in the middle of the road – were some of the advantages of motoring in a more leisurely age.

Pass of Kintraw

Kilmartin, c.1905. A wide range of prehistoric remains is represented in Lorn. The landscape around the village has a rich variety of evidence indicating human occupation from earliest times. The church has crosses dating from the ninth or tenth century and an important collection of medieval grave slabs. Visitors interested in archaeology and in landscape interpretation should make straight for the excellent museum at Kilmartin House. Controversy surrounds the Glebe Pot (2000 BC) currently held by the National Museum of Scotland in Edinburgh. Understandably, Kilmartin House is seeking to have this unique artefact returned for display; the cairn from which it was excavated in 1864 lies just a few yards from the museum's windows.

DUNADD HILL NEAR BELLANOCH.   219456.J.V.

According to the Irish Annalists, three royal princes from Ulster sailed up the River Add and made landfall at Dunadd in AD 498. Fergus Mor MacErca and his brothers Lorn and Angus were Scots (Irish Celts), and they apportioned much of the land we know as Argyll between them, occupying the seaboard opposite their own Emerald Isle. Such beginnings led to the foundation of Dalriada, an ancient kingdom whose boundaries stretched from Lochaber to the Mull of Kintyre and included part of Mull, Jura, Islay and the northern part of Ireland; Dunadd became the seat of these kings of Dalriada. Their arrival here was not surprising; long established trade routes by land and sea converged near Crinan – and most significantly – the Kintyre coast could be glimpsed from Ulster.

The craggy rock of Dunadd rises to a height of 176 feet above the low-lying plain of Mhòine Mhór – (the 'Great Moss') through which the River Add meanders to enter the sea at Crinan. Fifteen hundred years ago, the landscape was probably somewhat different as Loch Awe then drained westwards, and the newcomers may have made their way over a shallow sea to the very portals of Dunadd where, before the Moss was drained, a rocky area was traditionally a landing-place. On the hill, access to the former settlement is gained by a natural cleft in the rock. Excavations in 1902 and 1929 revealed Dunadd to have been both a fortress (having several self-contained defences), and also, from the range and quality of artefacts uncovered, a permanent settlement. Significant features include rock carvings in ogham script and the representation of a wild boar. A faint barefoot print and the impression of a large, hollowed footprint cut one inch deep appear to be marks of sovereignty. Such footprints are known to have played a part in inaugural ceremonies or coronations elsewhere, the chief or king placing his foot in the rock imprint to signify the assumption of dominion over his land. Other finds suggest that Christianity penetrated this very spot, and indeed, St Columba, Abbot of Iona, carried out the first Christian installation of a king in Britain when he consecrated Aidan, son of Gabhran, as King of Dalriada in AD 574.

History loses sight of Dunadd in the eighth century. In attempting to peer down the length of fifteen centuries and part the mists obscuring the hill at Dunadd, there is much about which we can only speculate. However, on one fact historians seem generally agreed: this place, the centre of the Dalriadan Kingdom, was Scotland's first capital.